T0371981

NAVIGATION DESIGN AND SEO FOR CONTENT-INTENSIVE WEBSITES

CHANDOS

INFORMATION PROFESSIONAL SERIES

Series Editor: Ruth Rikowski
(email: Rikowskigr@aol.com)

Chandos' new series of books is aimed at the busy information professional. They have been specially commissioned to provide the reader with an authoritative view of current thinking. They are designed to provide easy-to-read and (most importantly) practical coverage of topics that are of interest to librarians and other information professionals. If you would like a full listing of current and forthcoming titles, please visit www.chandospublishing.com.

New authors: We are always pleased to receive ideas for new titles; if you would like to write a book for Chandos, please contact Dr Glyn Jones on g.jones.2@elsevier.com or telephone +44 (0) 1865 843000.

NAVIGATION DESIGN AND SEO FOR CONTENT-INTENSIVE WEBSITES

A Guide for an Efficient Digital Communication

MARIO PÉREZ-MONTORO
LLUÍS CODINA

ELSEVIER

AMSTERDAM · BOSTON · HEIDELBERG · LONDON
NEW YORK · OXFORD · PARIS · SAN DIEGO
SAN FRANCISCO · SINGAPORE · SYDNEY · TOKYO

Chandos Publishing is an imprint of Elsevier

CP

CHANDOS
PUBLISHING

Chandos Publishing is an imprint of Elsevier
50 Hampshire Street, 5th Floor, Cambridge, MA 02139, USA
The Boulevard, Langford Lane, Kidlington, OX5 1GB, UK

Notices
Knowledge and best practice in this field are constantly changing. As new research and experience broaden our understanding, changes in research methods, professional practices, or medical treatment may become necessary.

Practitioners and researchers must always rely on their own experience and knowledge in evaluating and using any information, methods, compounds, or experiments described herein. In using such information or methods they should be mindful of their own safety and the safety of others, including parties for whom they have a professional responsibility.

To the fullest extent of the law, neither the Publisher nor the authors, contributors, or editors, assume any liability for any injury and/or damage to persons or property as a matter of products liability, negligence or otherwise, or from any use or operation of any methods, products, instructions, or ideas contained in the material herein.

British Library Cataloguing-in-Publication Data
A catalogue record for this book is available from the British Library

Library of Congress Cataloging-in-Publication Data
A catalog record for this book is available from the Library of Congress

ISBN: 978-0-08-100676-4 (print)
ISBN: 978-0-08-100677-1 (online)

For information on all Chandos Publishing publications
visit our website at https://www.elsevier.com/

Working together
to grow libraries in
developing countries

www.elsevier.com • www.bookaid.org

Publisher: Glyn Jones
Acquisition Editor: Glyn Jones
Editorial Project Manager: Harriet Clayton
Production Project Manager: Debasish Ghosh
Designer: Maria Ines Cruz

Typeset by TNQ Books and Journals

To our families

CONTENTS

LIST OF FIGURES

ABOUT THE AUTHORS

Dr. Mario Pérez-Montoro is an associate professor in the Department of Information Science and Media Studies, University of Barcelona, Spain, where he has taught in the areas of information architecture, interaction design, and information visualization for over 10 years. He is currently the Director of the PhD in Information and Communication Program at the University of Barcelona. Dr. Pérez-Montoro holds a PhD in philosophy and education from the University of Barcelona and a Master in Information Management and Systems from the Polytechnic University of Catalonia, Spain. He studied at the *Istituto di Discipline della Comunicazione* at the University of Bologna (Italy), he has been a professor at different universities in Spain (Complutense University of Madrid, Open University of Catalonia, and Autonomous University of Barcelona), and he has been visiting scholar at the Center for the Study of Language and Information (CSLI) at Stanford University (California, USA) and at the School of Information at UC Berkeley (California, USA).

Dr. Lluís Codina is an associate professor in the Department of Communication, at the School of Communication, Pompeu Fabra University, Spain, where he has taught information science courses in the areas of journalism and media studies for over 30 years. He is currently the Director of the Master in Social Communication Program at this university. He holds a PhD in journalism from the Autonomous University of Barcelona, Spain, where he was an assistant professor. Dr. Codina lectures in the Master on Online Documentation and Search Engine Optimization at the Institute of Long Live Learning of the Pompeu Fabra University, Spain. He is member of the Digital Documentation and Interactive Communication Research Group (DigiDoc), and director of its Research Seminar. He is the author of over 200 articles (in scientific journals and newspapers) and six books (as author or coauthor), in addition to various chapters in books.

ACKNOWLEDGMENT

This work has been made possible by funding of the project 'Active Audiences and Journalism. Interactivity, Web Integration and Findability of Journalistic Information'. CSO2012-39518-C04-02. National Plan for R + D + i, Spanish Ministry of Economy and Competitiveness.

CHAPTER 1

Content-Intensive Sites

1.1 INTRODUCTION

The main objective of this chapter is to introduce the concept of content-intensive Websites (or information-intensive Websites), since it is precisely this type of Website, and its content-heavy Web pages, to which the various concepts, ideas and techniques that we present in this book are best applied.

Next, we discuss the relationship between content-intensive Websites and the contributions made by library and information science to the universe of the World Wide Web. We conclude by providing a brief presentation of the overall content of this book, describing the subjects addressed in each of the remaining six chapters.

1.2 CHARACTERIZATION OF CONTENT-INTENSIVE SITES

Content-intensive sites (CISs) are characterized by the fact that they belong to organizations that *naturally* produce large volumes of information. That is, they produce this content not as a result of having to come up with strategies to fill their Website, as might be the case of other types of organization (we refer to the majority of firms operating in the business world, for example), but simply because they cannot *not* create it. In other words, they would cease to fulfil a fundamental part of their mission if they stopped creating content.

Generally speaking, there are three main types of organizations that present this characteristic: the media, universities and museums. We do not automatically rule out the possibility of there being other classes, but given the widespread presence of these three in any moderately developed society, their great social significance and their impact on knowledge, they are by far the most important.

The three types of institutions share a series of characteristics of enormous significance. First, the kind of information they produce and manage is of the broadest social interest and reach. Second, in their fields, they produce and manage information that enhances cultural quality and promotes the advancement of a nation's knowledge (and their coming together in an international system, of course, improves the cultural quality and promotes

Navigation Design and SEO for Content-Intensive Websites
ISBN 978-0-08-100676-4

the knowledge of mankind as a whole). Finally, in an era of unabated changes that can be traced to the beginning of the industrial revolution, they are three examples of centuries–old institutions that, despite suffering periodic crises, do not appear to be near the end of their existence; on the contrary, they would appear to be as strong as ever.

Briefly, the media provide the channels by which society, since at least the 18th century, has kept itself informed about what is going on around it and, since at least the beginning of the 20th century, it has been a formidable instrument in the defence of democracy in its role of keeping a watchful eye on those in power and, indeed, is often referred to as the 'fourth power'. Today, there is a widespread consensus that active, well–informed citizens thanks to a high-quality, free press are, in turn, the foundation of a strong democracy.

The universities, for their part, have been responsible, since the Middle Ages, for a dual function whose importance cannot be exaggerated: the dissemination of knowledge and the creation of new knowledge. As if this were not enough, they house the great university libraries, or as is preferred in more modern circles, resource centres for learning and research.

Finally, the museums, in existence since the beginning of the 18th century, fulfil the function of the preservation of our tangible and intangible cultural heritage and of making it available not only to researchers and scholars but to society as a whole. Their permanent collections form a massive archive whose digitization and documentation represent an invaluable and, fortunately, vast source of information and knowledge.

While to an outside observer of the world of both search engine optimization (SEO) and the library and information sciences, these three types of organizations might appear to have little in common, we would claim (summing up what we have said so far) that they are institutions that share a number of important characteristics. First, all three are deeply rooted in their respective societies. Second, they generate a wide variety of information as part of their natural activities. Third, their information is of broad social interest. They also generate multimedia information, that is, they produce content covering the entire spectrum of information morphologies (text, image, sound and video); and, more recently, they have begun to generate interactive content, linked even to augmented and virtual realities. Finally, all three are heavily conditioned to ensure that their contents are of quality and meet essential requirements of validity.

These characteristics endow the three institutions with an essential difference in relation to aspects of information architecture and of SEO. They all produce content of high semantic and cognitive value. Indeed, the multimedia information characteristic of the news media, universities and museums is extremely rich in semantic features and presents a significant cognitive dimension because it affects the higher-level functions of our cognition: the monitoring of what is going on around us, our artistic and scientific heritage and the generation and dissemination of knowledge.

Having said that, we should stress that the three categories do not exhaust the list of such sites, and that it is by no means a closed list. The sites form a set that cannot be defined by its extension but only by a certain affinity and, therefore, we cannot hope to provide a fixed list of sites that belong to this set.

CISs contrast most markedly with the sites of small- and medium-sized 'conventional' e-commerce firms and with most informational Websites for the products and services of companies of all sizes. However, the distinction we draw between e-commerce sites, on the one hand, and CISs, on the other, is imperfect, because as we show that there is an increasing number of e-commerce sites that share many of the features of CISs.

1.2.1 Mixed Systems

Having outlined what we consider to be the 'pure' category of CISs, we should hasten to clarify that there are systems in e-commerce that share many of their features.

These are Websites that go beyond the conventional e-commerce site or informational site for the products and services of a firm. We believe that there is a wide variety of such sites, and that the current business trend to move increasingly onto the Internet, or the cloud if you prefer, will mean that in the future these mixed sites, that is, originating in e-commerce but rich in content, will increase in number.

Examples of such sites include commercial image banks, such as those of the well-known firms Getty and Corbis, film and television databases, such as IMDB and AllMovie, and even global companies (in all senses) such as Amazon, and even large sector companies, such as Barnes & Noble.

Clearly all, or most, of what we might say about 'pure' CISs is applicable to these mixed sites, as we refer to them here. In both cases, we are dealing with sites that handle large volumes of content, most of it cognitive in type (be it image, text or audiovisual), that they need to produce as part of their natural functions or as part of their business model.

Given this gradual convergence, in this book when we refer to CISs we also take into consideration these so-called mixed sites, since to almost all intents and purposes they can be deemed equals for the subjects we discuss.

1.3 AN OPPORTUNITY FOR LIBRARY AND INFORMATION SCIENCE

From the perspective of library and information science (LIS), CISs and mixed sites are of great interest because they both require intense inputs from this field of study.

The reason for this is that LIS does not concern itself with just any kind of information. Indeed, information is the subject of study and the focus of many disciplines and professions. Biology, for example, is concerned with information (among other things) when it studies the laws of genetics, and so is mass communication, to choose a discipline at the other end of the academic spectrum, when it examines the messages circulating in the media.

Information is an ever-present facet in the life experience of human beings as individuals and also of human societies as a whole. People constantly exchange information with each other as part of their vital interaction with their fellow man. Society deals with huge amounts of information on a permanent basis and in real time, including, for example, city traffic and pollution data.

What exactly is the focus of interest of LIS in this overwhelming panorama presided over by the constant exchange of information? We believe that by examining our specific object of study we are able to recognize a number of characteristics that are at the same time unique and exclusive to the information that concerns us in the field of LIS.

First, LIS does not concern itself with just any kind of information, as we have been at pains to illustrate with the previous examples; rather, it concerns itself with information that is recorded in material supports, what we can refer to as documents.

For many years now LIS has not only focused its attention on printed documents and textual information. As mentioned, the concept of the document includes any kind of recorded material including digital supports and all types of information morphology, including text, image, video and sound. This means that LIS is not only concerned with monographs and articles in print magazines housed in libraries but also with computer records hosted in database systems.

Second, LIS does not concern itself with administrative information, such as that produced daily by millions of businesses and individuals around the globe, which means the balance sheets of a country's companies are not to be found in libraries; rather, we have to visit the company archives or the nation's historical archives (if the information is old) to find them.

The information that LIS does concern itself with, therefore, is what we might call cognitive information. This class of information, in contrast with administrative information, is to be found in the monographs and magazines acquired, catalogued and made available to the general public in centres such as libraries, as well as by the compilers of databases and other organizations in the world of LIS.

What is important for us is that CISs need to make full use of the intellectual and technological tools provided by LIS. By this we mean that the concepts and procedures presented in this book only acquire their full meaning in the context of CISs.

As modern content management systems (CMSs) have made manifest, information architecture design and the need to employ taxonomies are trivial concerns. The so-called predesigned themes with menus based on categories and tags, developed by the most important CMSs, can solve most of the problems that might affect a standard site, using well-established patterns.

The same cannot be said, however, for CISs and for content-rich sites similar to the CISs. Given their characteristics, these sites have a number of specific needs in relation to the concepts and ideas addressed in this book, which, in contrast, are not applicable to a classic e-commerce site or a typical content-poor site of a business or firm.

1.4 HOW THE BOOK IS STRUCTURED

In this book, it is our understanding that information architecture (IA) (via its contribution to the design of navigation systems) and SEO occupy a privileged place in their applications to CISs (see the reasons outlined before). Likewise, we believe both IA and SEO occupy privileged places in the applications of LIS to the universe of the web.

In keeping with these beliefs, we can build an interesting triangle, with one side being formed by the World Wide Web, the second by LIS and the third by the partnership forged between AI + SEO. It is precisely this triangle that has served as our motivation to work and research in these areas at our respective universities, and it is these ideas that we now wish to make available in this book.

In Chapter 2, we analyse the bases on which the navigation system is founded and that allow a user to explore and locate information in web environments and on mobile devices. To do so, we organize the chapter into four sections. Firstly, we examine the subject of navigation in fairly broad terms. Specifically, the section begins by highlighting the basic importance of navigation and how this is manifest in web environments. We follow this by offering a complete definition of the navigation system. Finally, we round off the section by providing a series of recommendations (or heuristics) that can be followed to improve the design and implementation of a Website navigation system.

In the second section of this chapter, we show how the overall navigation system that can be found on a webpage is usually built up from different elements or subsystems. We examine this typology and describe the two basic navigation systems: embedded systems – constant, local and contextual systems; and supplementary systems – maps, indexes and guides. In the third section, we present the advanced or nonbasic systems – personalization systems, visual navigation systems and social navigation systems. And, in the fourth section, we examine the components that enable us to add extra layers of semantic navigation to a site and that enhance both the user's navigating experience and the site's SEO.

In Chapter 3, we focus our attention on describing and analysing methodological questions associated with the implementation of navigation.

The first section is dedicated to examining the different phases or stages that have to be completed to ensure our navigation resources are designed efficiently. Specifically, we focus on the stages of analysis, design and implementation. The analysis stage examines in detail the scenario in which the site will be developed and includes contextual, content and user analyses. In the design phase, we present the navigation resources and develop a content inventory and content models, a representation of the vocabulary, the prototype and an evaluation of the proposed navigation system. Finally, in the implementation phase, an initial version of the navigation system that was drawn up in the design phase is developed, and this is then communicated before the eventual Website is developed and the style guides created.

The next two sections are dedicated to addressing two of the most frequently used methodological strategies of user analysis, developed to ensure the efficient design of navigation resources: the persona–scenario method and the card sorting technique. The persona–scenario method is a nonparticipatory analysis technique that seeks both to identify the site's target users and to place their actions within a given context, thus allowing decisions to be taken about the design and structure of our project. The card sorting technique is a participatory methodological strategy that allows us to design different (constant and local) navigation systems drawing on the cognitive organizations presented by the site's target users.

Chapter 4 has two aims: first, to analyse the functions of prototyping and prototyping typologies and, second, to describe and review a series of online and desktop tools designed to facilitate the creation of prototypes for the design and creation of Web pages and digital content for mobile devices. To meet these goals, the chapter is organized as follows. First, we begin by outlining the importance and functionality of prototyping for the architectural design of a Website. Then, we analyse the two main types of prototypes or diagrams typically used to represent the architecture proposed for a webpage: blueprints and wireframes. Finally, we review some of the main (online and desktop) solutions for developing and implementing Website diagramming or prototyping.

Introducing the essentials of SEO or Website positioning is the main objective of Chapter 5. Here, we examine the basic guidelines and best practices that ensure a Website is visible on the World Wide Web. First, we present a brief description of SEO from the point of view of its main objectives. Then we focus on one of its principal objects of study, search engines, to understand how they analyse and interpret information, and how they rank it on their results pages. Finally, in this chapter, we look at Website positioning factors by grouping them in two sets, the on-site and off-site.

Having reviewed the essentials of SEO, in Chapter 6 we present the different phases of a positioning campaign, then move on to focus our attention on aspects of OnSite SEO and, in particular, on content-based SEO, as this is one of the strengths of CISs. Specifically, we introduce the main phases of an SEO campaign. But once these phases of the campaign have been implemented, the only way to sustain the site's position is by promoting a continuous policy of content creation and publishing.

To meet this objective, we also present a framework proposal to optimize site content linked to the production of news and current affairs, given that this is one of the most characteristic cases of CISs. However, this proposal can be extended to all the other CISs that we refer to throughout this book (that is, not only news media sites but also university and museum Websites).

In the preceding chapters we therefore examine, first, the essentials of SEO and, second, the phases of an optimization campaign as well as a framework for optimizing the production of a CIS, taking as our example a media communication site, although the recommendations we make can be extrapolated to other CISs.

Finally, in Chapter 7, we first review the current state of the mobile web, considering a range of different devices based on their screen size, given that this characteristic is the main determinant of the user experience. We also consider mobile operating systems and applications, in particular, news aggregators. Finally, we link SEO and the mobile web via both searches and responsive web design, first introduced in Chapter 2.

PART ONE

Navigation Experience Design

CHAPTER 2

The Basis of Navigation

2.1 INTRODUCTION

Navigation systems are one of the most important systems or structures making up the anatomy of information architecture for Website design.

Along with search systems, navigation systems are the most frequently used architectural structures of a Website for locating and accessing the information it contains. Usually, the first thing a user does when opening a webpage is to explore its content using the labels that make up the site's navigation system.

In this chapter we analyze the bases on which the navigation system is founded and that allow a user to explore and locate information in web environments and on mobile devices.

To do so, we organize the chapter into four sections. In the first (Section 2.2) we examine the subject of navigation in fairly broad terms. Specifically, the section begins by highlighting the basic importance of navigation and how this is manifest in web environments. We follow this up by offering a complete definition of the navigation system. Finally, we round off the section by providing a series of recommendations (or heuristics) that can be followed to improve the design and implementation of a Website navigation system.

In Section 2.3, the chapter shows how the overall navigation system that can be found on a webpage is usually built up from different elements or subsystems. In the first two subsections, we examine this typology and describe the two basic navigation systems: embedded systems – constant, local and contextual systems; and supplementary systems – maps, indexes and guides. And, finally, in the last subsection, we present the advanced or nonbasic systems – personalization systems, visual navigation systems and social navigation systems.

In Section 2.4, we examine the components that enable us to add extra layers of semantic navigation to a site and that enhance both the user's navigating experience and the site's search engine optimization (SEO).

The chapter concludes in Section 2.5 with examination of various navigation phenomena in the context of mobile devices (smartphones, tablets and laptop hybrids). To do so, we first describe the patterns that are used to

Navigation Design and SEO for Content-Intensive Websites
ISBN 978-0-08-100676-4

navigate web content from a mobile device. And, second, in the last subsection, we present the different navigation systems or patterns (primary and secondary) that the applications (apps) of these devices incorporate to facilitate their use.

2.2 DIGITAL NAVIGATION

Navigation systems in web environments can be considered as being one of the most common structures in the anatomy of the site's information architecture and, along with search systems, one of the most frequently employed for locating the information that can satisfy users' needs.

Bearing these characteristics in mind, and to describe and analyze systems of this type, in this section we seek to highlight the general importance of navigation and how it manifests itself in web environments. We provide a complete definition of the navigation system and offer some general recommendations that can help in the design and implementation of such systems.

2.2.1 Importance

Broadly speaking, since the dawn of humanity, man has needed to orientate himself as he journeys from place to place. To satisfy this need, he has been able to develop various tools to find his way around and to ensure that he safely reaches his chosen destination.

Usually these tools have consisted of small visual representations drawn to scale, a model in which the main relief features of the journey, or the territory he intends to cross, are depicted. These tools offered obvious advantages; at any point during the journey, they served as a system of orientation for the traveller, allowing him to know where he had come from, where he was, the direction in which he should continue his journey and how to reach his chosen destination. The map is the obvious example of tools of this type.

In web environments, this need for orientation is, if anything, even greater. To take full advantage of the contents hung on a large Website, it is imperative that we quickly orientate ourselves as we try to find the information it contains. Being lost can lead to feelings of confusion and frustration, and even result in a user abandoning the Website. Ultimately, quitting a site, even though it has useful, interesting content, can be seen as an indication that the site is of little or no value.

In contexts of this kind, navigation systems are the main architectural structures providing us with the resources to help locate information. This type of system in the context of a webpage, like the maps we use on our journeys in the real world, allows us to orientate ourselves and to know where we are, what we can find in this place, the route we took in coming here and how we can get to where we want to be.

2.2.2 Definition

Technically speaking, navigation (or exploration) systems are architectural structures that sort and group Website content into different categories within a broader classification. This sorting and grouping is intentionally designed to fulfil a number of important goals. On the one hand, it allows the user to identify the relationships between the content hosted on a Website and the relationships between that content and the page or site that the user is currently visiting. On the other hand, it enables and facilitates navigation between these contents. In other words, it enables assisted, controlled navigation through the different sections and pages that make up the Website; it provides a system or method of orientation so that users can navigate in a controlled way from one point of the Website to another, knowing at all times where they are, what they can find there, where they came from and where they can go. Clearly, the navigation system is designed to facilitate the user's location of information and, therefore, to make the Website as useful as possible. The last objective it pursues is to offer the user the possibility of acquiring, albeit indirectly through interaction with this structure, an idea or mental image of the size and structure of the Website itself.

To facilitate the location of information, navigation systems use the navigation or exploration technique. This technique involves the choosing of a general category, and then by activating links, moving toward increasingly more specific materials until the user reaches the category that corresponds most closely to his needs and where he can find the content he has been looking for. This strategy requires a high degree of intellectual activity on the part of the user as he has to choose between the different categories that the system makes available to him. Each system uses its own categories and its own hierarchical levels. Such systems are especially useful for trying to locate general information about a given subject or information that belongs to a distinct category, in stable and well-structured sources of information.

2.2.3 General Heuristics

Having outlined, albeit schematically, the importance of architectural structures of this type and defined just what a navigation system is, we can now offer a series of recommendations (or heuristics) that can be followed to improve the process of design and implementation of a webpage navigation system.

The advice or recommendations we want to offer are related to the following areas: contextualization resources, browser consistency and navigation design.

2.2.3.1 Contextualization Resources

As we have pointed out, when designing a webpage it is important to bear in mind that the users, if they are going to be able to exploit the information it contains properly, need to know where they are at all times and where they can go to as they begin to explore the Website.

Unfortunately, unlike in the physical world, there are no relief features (mountains, rivers, trees, streets, monuments, underground stations, buildings etc.) in web environments that can help users orientate themselves within a Website. For this reason, it is critical that all the pages making up a Website are contextualized and that they indicate at all times, by means of contextualization resources or cues, the relationship between their content and the Website that houses it (Evans, 1998; Farkas & Farkas, 2000; IBM, 1999; Lynch & Horton, 2009; Marchionini, 1995; Nielsen & Tahir, 2002; Spool, Scanlon, Schroeder, Snyder, & DeAngelo, 1997, among others). In short, offering these contextualization resources or cues is, so to speak, a way of applying the wayfinding discipline to web environments (Wodtke, 2009).

There are two main ways of providing these contextualization resources or cues: by providing a logo and by presenting aspects of the hierarchy visually.

In the case of the first option, one of the most common ways of providing these resources is by embedding the logo or the name of the organization that usually appears on the homepage in each of the chunks of content that hang from this page. This strategy allows users to know where they are; it also allows those users that have reached the page via a search engine or an external link, and who have therefore bypassed the homepage, to know where they are. An example of such a strategy is presented in Fig. 2.1, on the homepage of University of Barcelona. As we can see, on the homepage and in all the content hung there, the logo (the crest in this case) of the university always appears, top right, in the same location.

Figure 2.1 University of Barcelona (www.ub.edu).

The second of the contextualization options is to show, via the system of navigation or exploration, the hierarchical structure that exists between the content and, at the same time, to show users where they are in the Website with respect to that hierarchy. This is usually done in two different ways: using visual cues to show the path from the homepage to the page that the user is on, or by explicitly giving the path, route or cue from the homepage to the page the user is on.

In the first case, a series of highly intuitive visualization resources are introduced that, in one way or another, enable users to identify the path taken in browsing and navigating from the homepage. An example of this type of visual resource (highlighted in red boxes) can be found in Fig. 2.2. In Fig. 2.2, which reproduces the homepage of Barcelona Contemporary Culture Centre, we can see how the navigation route taken when exploring the Website from the homepage is recorded: we first clicked on 'Activities' (text colour variation being the visual aid used) and we then clicked on 'Audiovisuals' (with the sign 'x' being the visual aid here).

In the second case, the explicit or textual path or route is given from the homepage to the page that the user is on. This resource is also known as 'breadcrumbs', inspired by the Brothers Grimm tale in which the children, Hansel and Gretel, use bread crumbs to mark out the route they have taken so they can find their way home every time they are abandoned in the woods.

Figure 2.2 Barcelona Contemporary Culture Centre (www.cccb.org).

Figure 2.3 University of Barcelona (www.ub.edu).

The breadcrumbs are usually placed top left, under the page heading, and immediately before the page's main content. An example of this resource can be found on the University of Barcelona's homepage (Fig. 2.3). As we can see, highlighted in red, this page shows the path we have followed since we began to navigate the homepage: we first clicked on 'The University', then 'Campuses, faculties and departments', and, finally, 'Faculties and schools'.

Including a breadcrumb system on a webpage offers significant benefits. First, it helps users orientate themselves when navigating or exploring the Website, providing them with information about where they are and how they got there. Second, the system also helps improve the Website's efficiency as far as the location of information is concerned. This system provides short-cuts so users can go straight back to previously visited pages (by activating or clicking on the links that appear or that form part of the trail or itinerary) without having to use the browser's back button, the navigation bar or the search system. And, by providing these shortcuts, users do not have to visit so many pages to locate the information they are seeking and, so, they take less time to find it. Finally, the system also helps users to construct a mental model of the Website thus reducing any feelings of disorientation once inside. Breadcrumbs, by offering a textual representation of the Website structure, allow users to obtain a representation of the navigation system's most impor-tant categories and of the semantic dependencies that exist between them.

So that this type of system can provide these benefits and contribute positively to the correct development of a webpage's navigation system, it should not be designed as a substitute for other navigation systems, and steps should be taken to ensure that each of the elements making up the bread-crumbs are links so that users can navigate via them.

Three different types of breadcrumb systems can be identified: location, path and attribute breadcrumbs (Instone, 2009; Gube, 2009, among others).

Location breadcrumbs are linked primarily to the architectural structure of the Website. This type of system tells us about the place, within the site, where the page currently being viewed is located; however, this is indepen-dent of the user's prior navigation. These breadcrumbs are usually constructed in a fixed, unchanged form and are defined independently of any possible user movements. These breadcrumbs are used on webpages with a static informational structure, where every element or content occupies a separate place. They can be used to answer the question: Where is this page that I am now visiting? An example of this system can be found on the University of Barcelona's Website (Fig. 2.4). In this figure we show the two breadcrumbs generated following our navigation from the homepage (highlighted in red boxes). The figure in the background shows how we have activated the link 'Studying and Teaching' and how the first breadcrumb ('Home > Studies') is generated. Then, from this same culture page we have activated the link 'The University' and generated a new or a second breadcrumb ('Home >The University') that does not show our navigation route but simply reflects the location of the page visited with respect to the homepage.

Figure 2.4 University of Barcelona (www.ub.edu).

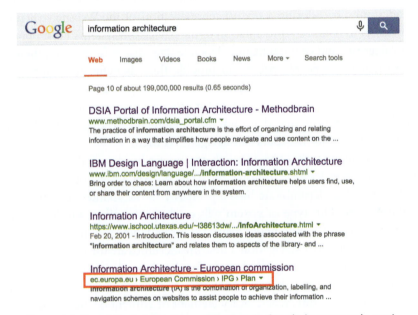

Figure 2.5 Search for information architecture in Google (www.google.com).

Interestingly, even Google is incorporating this type of resource into its browser. When we enter a search equation, Google usually offers us a series of results, highlighting, among other things, the title, a brief description and the URL of the site retrieved. If the site retrieved incorporates a breadcrumb system, Google tries to reflect this in the site URL provided on the results page. As Fig. 2.5 shows, with some of the results proposed for the search equation 'information architecture' (the fourth, for example, highlighted by a red rectangle), Google provides us with the URL of the page retrieved, including the breadcrumb trail that leads from the site's homepage to the page retrieved. The advantages of using resources of this type are clearly apparent. On the one hand, by including breadcrumbs, the resource or page URL can be more readily interpreted by users, since it gives information about the sections in which that resource can be retrieved. In our example, the result indicates, among other things, that the resource retrieved is a plan within a section devoted to information providers guides (IPGs). On the other hand, it explicitly tells users which branch of the hierarchical structure the page or resource retrieved is embedded in, without their having to visit and browse the site that houses it in order to retrieve it. In our example, it allows us to know that the resource retrieved is embedded in the hierarchical branch 'European Commission'>'IPG'>'Plan' that structures the site that houses it. And, finally, it also activates the links that make up the breadcrumbs so that we can directly access other pages on the Website that host the resource retrieved and that can help meet our information needs.

Path breadcrumbs, in contrast, are linked primarily to the user's prior navigation trail. This type of system also tells the user where they are, although its main objective is to show the path, route or itinerary taken by the user to access the content displayed. Unlike location breadcrumbs, they are built from the user's actual navigation. Systems of this type are typically used in Websites with a dynamic data structure, in which each element might be located in different places and where there are alternative paths to access them. They can be used to answer the question: How did I get here? An example of this second type of breadcrumb trail is provided in Fig. 2.6 showing a newspaper's Website. Here, highlighted in a red box, we show the navigation path taken from the homepage: first, we visited the Tech section; from there we visited the Opinion section, followed by the Life section and the Sport section, finishing in the NBA section.

Finally, attribute breadcrumbs are linked primarily to the information contained on the webpage being visited. This type of system provides meta-information about the page the user accessed. Like location breadcrumbs, they are independent of the user's navigation. They can be used to answer the question: What contents correspond to a particular characteristic? An example of attribute breadcrumbs can be found in the Dmoz directory page (Fig. 2.7). There we entered the search equation navigation design. As can be seen in the highlighted red boxes, after executing the search, for each result the page shows us the path we could have followed to reach each of the result pages if instead of using the search system we had browsed the

Figure 2.6 Example of path breadcrumb.

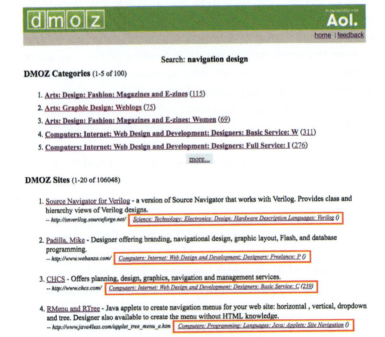

Figure 2.7 Dmoz directory page (https://www.dmoz.org).

directory's categories, offering us additional information about the contents of the pages retrieved.

2.2.3.2 *Browser Consistency*

When designing a navigation system, it should be borne in mind that it will have to work through a browser and, therefore, attempts must be made to maintain a certain degree of consistency with the browser.

A browser is a tool that allows a webpage to be accessed and viewed. Explorer, Safari, Chrome and Mozilla Firefox are all examples of such tools.

Browsers allow users to perform various actions when trying to locate information on the Internet. Thus, for example, they allow direct access to a webpage via its address or URL. Activating the back and forward buttons gives the user access to the previous page or the last page visited. They also provide a menu of the user's browsing history displaying the pages that have been visited. The 'favourites' option enables the user to store the addresses of pages of special interest so they can be readily visited in the future. Taking advantage of the links, browsers also provide access to content that is related to the page visited.

It is interesting to note that these links change colour if we have visited them previously (Evans, 1998; Nielsen & Tahir, 2002; Nielsen, 1996, 1999a, 1999b, 2003; Spool et al., 2001; Tullis, 2001, among others) and that when we move the mouse over the text link, the address of the content we can access is displayed. An example of the implementation of this first recommendation can be found on the Nautilus Website (Fig. 2.8). Here we can see how the link 'My Family, My Science' changes colour once it has been activated. In Fig. 2.9, we find an example of the implementation of the second recommendation. If you hover over the link itself, we can see how the browser provides us with the address (lower left) of the chosen content.

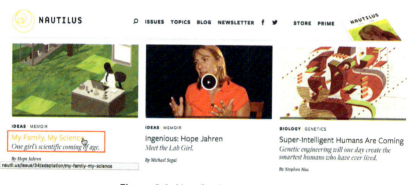

Figure 2.8 Nautilus (www.nautil.us).

Figure 2.9 Nautilus (www.nautil.us).

The typical browser inconsistency errors made when building a page are usually associated with the very functions that the browser itself facilitates. For example, it is common to find Websites in which the colour codes of the links visited do not change; in which the 'favourites' option is badly mutilated; in which the address of the linked content is not displayed when the mouse hovers over the text link that connects it; and in which the option to use the directional buttons to access pages already visited, and so exploit the navigation route taken to locate previously identified information, is not possible when content is opened on a new page (Detweiler & Omanson, 1996; Evans, 1998; Lynch & Horton, 2009; Nielsen & Tahir, 2002; Spool et al., 1997; Tullis, 2001; Zimmerman, Slater & Kendall, 2001).

2.2.3.3 Navigation Design

Finally, we present some general recommendations for navigation design to ensure these structures are properly constructed.

The first general recommendations are fairly intuitive. Thus, for example, it is a good idea to include a web map (accessible from the homepage) that serves to orientate users, but efforts should be made not to overload the homepage with too many labels and navigation techniques (Nielsen, 2009). Alternatively, on a separate page, some kind of navigation guide might be developed for the most common information needs of the visitors to that page.

Another useful recommendation is, where necessary, to include drop-down menus. These cascading menus can be used when there is little space to display many links since, on activating a label in the navigation system, they can show a list of items. Although they allow many different

Figure 2.10 Pompeu Fabra University (www.upf.edu).

options to be concentrated in very little space, they have the disadvantage that until they are opened the user does not know what options are available. To reduce the amount of time and the number of errors in their use, some authors argue that it is preferable that they open up when activated and stay open rather than only showing the individual options available when passing the mouse over them (Chaparro, Minnaert, & Phipps, 2000). An example of drop-down menus can be found on the homepage of Pompeu Fabra University (Fig. 2.10). As illustrated, when activating the 'University' label in the navigation bar, a menu drops down to offer the user different options.

On the other hand, it should be borne in mind that both content size and structure play a critical role in the design of navigation systems and in their correct use. In the case of size, a small content facilitates the establishment of links, while a large content allows a greater amount of information with different structures to be expressed. In the case of structure, content that presents a certain uniformity with respect to the distribution and internal architecture facilitates user orientation, while unstructured content allows the representation of information in any format. Maintaining a balance between the size and degree of structuring of the content is the most common recommendation made in these cases, although we should not lose sight of the fact that both the type of content and the users' information needs can justify the introduction of small changes in this balanced proposal.

Finally, when designing a suitable navigation system, and above all, when choosing the labels to use in it, it is highly advisable to bear the concept of information scent (or the information footprint) in mind. The expression 'information scent' is a term used to describe how users evaluate the options available to them when trying to locate information on a Website (Backer, 2005). When presented with a list of options, users choose the one that offers the clearest indication (or the strongest scent), ie, the one that will lead them directly to the information they seek. In quantitative terms, this concept should be understood as the extent to which the label of a link is representative of the information of the content to which it points, as a measure for calculating the degree of expressiveness of the text link (Katz & Byrne, 2003).

The trail concept is based on the extended metaphor of information foraging (Pirolli & Card, 1995). It is an ecological term that seeks to explain human adaptation to information flow in the same terms as those used to explain how living things adapt to their environment biologically. Thus, the behaviour of humans when searching for information is comparable to that presented by hunters tracking their prey, or that of gatherers looking for food or that of any animal setting out to find food in order to survive. We locate information on webpages in the same way as predators and hunters scour the earth in search of the clearest tracks that will lead them directly to their kill.

This ecological way of addressing the functionality of links has been applied and extended to all contexts in which a link might be involved. For example, studies have been conducted in which a link acts as an index (Pirolli & Card, 1995) and cases have been examined in which graphics are included that incorporate a web link (Pirolli, Card, & Van Der Wege, 2000), in which an icon has been used as a link (Chi, Pirolli, Chen, & Pitkow, 2001) and in which web links are used as titles that describe the content of the text to which they link up (Card et al., 2001). However, the problem with these studies of information trails is that they typically measure this trail with respect to a specific task or set of tasks; they do not attempt to measure it for each link in absolute terms, which prevents us from inferring any general laws from this body of work that might help us improve the trail of links in all types of context.

2.3 NAVIGATION SYSTEM TYPOLOGY

The general navigation system usually found on a Website tends to be formed from a combination of different elements or subsystems: the basic navigation systems and the nonbasic navigation systems (Morville, Rosenfeld, & Arango, 2015).

Basic systems		Non-basic systems
Embedded systems	Supplementary systems	Personalization navigation systems
Constant systems	Site maps	Visual navigation systems
Local systems	Indexes	Social navigation systems
Contextual systems	Guides	

Figure 2.11 Navigation system typology.

Basic navigation systems are the exploration systems that most webpages implement. These systems, in turn, are formed from a combination of embedded navigation systems and supplementary navigation systems. Embedded systems include constant, local and contextual navigation systems, while complementary systems bring together site maps, indexes and guides.

Advanced navigation systems (or nonbasic navigation systems), in contrast, are not usually implemented on webpages but rather are used as exploration systems for specific Websites. These systems tend to combine personalization and customization systems, visual navigation systems and social navigation systems.

To examine the navigation system typology, the next section is structured as follows. In Subsections 2.3.1 and 2.3.2 we describe the basic navigation systems (the embedded systems – constant, local and contextual systems) and the supplementary systems (maps, indexes and guides), respectively. In Subsection 2.3.3, we present the nonbasic or advanced systems (personalization systems, visual navigation systems and social navigation systems). A general overview of this classification of the navigation systems that can make up a webpage is provided in Fig. 2.11.

2.3.1 Embedded Navigation Systems

Embedded navigation systems, along with supplementary systems, form part of the basic navigation systems that are usually implemented on most of the webpages that a user might access.

In addition to being widely implemented, the main characteristic of embedded navigation systems is that they literally form part of the architectural structure of the Website pages that incorporate them. Moreover, they provide the main information that users need to find their way around the site: where they are, what content is located near to the page being visited, what content is related to the content they are currently accessing and where they might go from this content-bearing page.

The main types of embedded navigation systems to be found on a webpage are the constant, local and contextual navigation systems.

2.3.1.1 Constant Navigation Systems

Constant navigation systems (or global navigation systems, to use the terminology proposed by Morville et al., 2015) tend to be incorporated into almost all the pages making up a Website. They usually appear as a horizontal navigation bar at the top of each page. An example of this type of navigation system can be found on the homepage of The Verge, highlighted by the red box in Fig. 2.12.

Navigation systems of this type offer users a system of orientation that allows them to know where they are at all times and where they can go to from the page being visited. They usually allow access to the most important content-bearing pages on the Website. They do not usually reflect the structural hierarchy between the content of a particular page or specific content, although they do provide an idea of how the overall Website is structured. As systems of this type have a direct impact on the usability of the site in which they are incorporated, they are usually subject to numerous tests and trials before finally being included within that Website.

Normally it is recommended that constant navigation systems appear centred at the top of the page (Badre, 2002; Bernard, 2001, 2002; Byrne, Anderson, Douglass, & Matessa, 1999; Ehret, 2002; Hornof & Halverson, 2003); however, some studies claim that they are more efficient for the user if located in a column to the left of the page and if they include the navigation system's second- and third-level selection structures (Kalbach, 2007; Kingsburg & Andre, 2004). An example of this latter strategy (with the navigational panel to the left) can be found on the homepage of Vox (Fig. 2.13).

Figure 2.12 The Verge (www.theverge.com).

Figure 2.13 Vox (www.vox.com).

As highlighted in the red box, on this page the navigation system is located in a column to the left.

This type of navigation system tends to include and repeat a fixed and specific series of labels or categories in most of the Websites that incorporate it. Among these labels, for example, we find the label that allows the user to return to the homepage from any content they are visiting and the label that allows them direct access to the search system.

Interestingly, the assumption of the three-click rule (no page on a Website should be more than three clicks away from the homepage or the opening page; or in other words, users should be able to access the information they need using no more than three clicks) associated with a site's usability means many information architects opt to build broad, shallow hierarchies rather than narrow, deep structures when designing a constant navigation system. Broad, shallow hierarchies offer more navigation options at the top and, therefore, short navigation sequences. This allows the three-click rule to be respected. Narrow, deep hierarchies, in contrast, offer few navigation options at the top of the hierarchy and, therefore, long navigation sequences. This means users have to violate the three-click rule when they are looking for something.

However, Porter (2003), based on an experiment with 44 users attempting 620 tasks and in which he analyzed more than 8000 clicks, demonstrated the three-click rule to be false. On the one hand, the experiment showed users were no more likely to abandon the site after three clicks than they were, for example, after 12 clicks. Hence, the number of clicks neither indicates nor predicts the success or failure of a task. Moreover, he also showed that the degree of user satisfaction does not depend on the number of clicks. Participants that had to activate fewer links did not report being more satisfied than those who had to activate a greater number. And, finally, he showed that when users find what they want, they do not complain about the number of clicks or links they had to activate; rather what is important for users is not the number of clicks they have had to make but whether or not they are able to locate what they want.

In a similar vein, various authors, including Krug (2000), for example, claim that the number of clicks a user has to make to find information is not important. What is important is that every click is meaningful and unambiguous. Moreover, broad, shallow hierarchies require greater cognitive effort as users have to choose from among all the options at the top of the hierarchy; while narrow, deep hierarchies, although they violate the three-click rule, require less cognitive effort as users have to choose between fewer options at the top of the hierarchy, and as these are activated the categories listed serve to disambiguate the label.

Finally, there is a current tendency to design these navigation systems in a rigid way guaranteeing their visibility at all times, regardless of the interaction with the user. This means that, to facilitate their use at all times, the system is visible even though the user has scrolled down the page. Examples of this design strategy can be found on the homepage of Nautilus (Fig. 2.14).

2.3.1.2 Local Navigation Systems

Local navigation systems, usually comprising a vertical navigation bar (although, on occasions, it might be designed horizontally), complement and articulate the constant systems. They are used to explore the specific page (and the content hung from it) of the Website that the user has accessed. These systems offer users a system of orientation that lets them know what content is located near the page they have accessed and where they can go from that content or page.

An example of this system can be found in Figs. 2.15 and 2.16. In Fig. 2.15, the local navigation system of the page dedicated to art collections (which can be accessed by activating the 'Collection' label in the constant

My Family, My Science
One girl's scientific coming of age.
By Hope Jahren

Ingenious: Hope Jahren
Meet the Lab Girl.
By Michael Segal

Super-Intelligent Humans Are Coming
Genetic engineering will one day create the smartest humans who have ever lived.
By Stephen Hsu

CULTURE SOCIOLOGY
Families of Choice Are Remaking America
Through their networks of friends, singles are strengthening society's social bonds.
By Bella DePaulo

Figure 2.14 Nautilus (www.nautil.us).

Figure 2.15 Smithsonian American Art Museum (americanart.si.edu).

Figure 2.16 University of Barcelona (www.ub.edu).

navigation system of the homepage of the Smithsonian American Art Museum) is in the column to the left (highlighted in the red box).

2.3.1.3 Contextual Navigation Systems

There are certain relationships between contents that escape the system or that cannot be captured by the constant and local navigation systems. Contextual navigation systems allow these relationships to be established and, thus, to complete the information offered to the user visiting a content-based page with that appearing on another page and that is related by using a link or hyperlink to it.

Contextual navigation systems are usually introduced with links or hyperlinks that use as their web link some part (text or image) of a page that connects with other content. An example of this type of link can be found on the page dedicated to admission at the University of Barcelona (see Fig. 2.16). On this page there are links that allow us to explore other content so that we can complete the information offered by this page. Thus, for example, the link 'Admission with foreign qualifications' takes us to a new page offering more information about this academic process.

As can be inferred from this example, this type of navigation system offers users a means of orientation that enables them to know what other information is related to the page or content they are visiting, where they can go from that page and how they can access this supplementary content (by clicking or activating the link).

The key to designing a good contextual navigation system lies in constructing hyperlinks that can properly orientate users seeking information so that they can complete the content of the page they are visiting. Following we consider the most important guidelines to ensure this objective is met.

The first point we want to emphasize is the need to establish reciprocal contextual links between related content appearing on different pages (Koyani & Nall, 1999). For example, on the Wikipedia page dedicated to Wittgenstein (see Fig. 2.17) there is a link ('Tractatus Logicus-Philosophicus') that leads to the Tractatus Logicus-Philosophicus page, and on that same page of Tractatus Logicus-Philosophicus there is another link ('Ludwig Josef Johann Wittgenstein') that allows you to access the Wittgenstein page.

Moreover, to guarantee user access, it is important to ensure that the web's critical content or pages receive links (even if these are repeated) from other different content-bearing pages (Bernard, Hull, & Drake, 2001; Detweiler & Omanson, 1996; Ivory, Sinha, & Hearst, 2000; Levine, 1996; Nall, Koyani, & Lafond, 2001; Nielsen & Tahir, 2002; Spain, 1999; Spool,

Figure 2.17 Wikipedia (en.wikipedia.org).

Klee, & Schroeder, 2000). An example of the implementation of this recommendation can be found on the Nautilus webpage (Fig. 2.18). As is highlighted in the red boxes, there, to increase subscriptions, the link 'Prime' (that gives you unlimited, ad-free reading of current and past issues, tablet editions of their award-winning print magazine, and eBook editions of every online issue) is repeated.

Another important point is to give visual cues so that the user can visually discriminate the link (a different colour from that of the rest of the text, underlining, etc.) on the page (Bailey, 2000; Bailey, Koyani, & Nall, 2000; Farkas & Farkas, 2000; Lynch & Horton, 2009; Nielsen, 1990; Tullis, 2001, among others). An example of this strategy can be found on the University of Barcelona's webpage (Fig. 2.19). As can be seen, the colour blue is used (and underlining when scrolled over) to highlight the links that can be activated.

Similarly, from the point of view of usability, to ensure that the potential visitor sees the links and accesses the information they contain, contextual links can be included as a fixed element and in the same position in the content hung on the Website (Nielsen, 2009). An example of this strategy can be found on the University of Barcelona's Website (Fig. 2.20). Here we can see how some of the links that facilitate contextual navigation (those that complete the text 'Further information') are located in the same

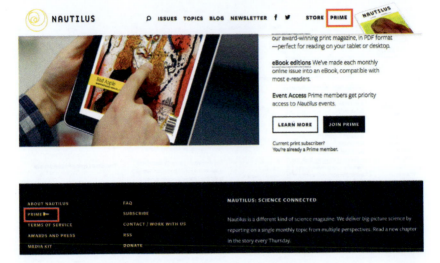

Figure 2.18 Nautilus (www.nautil.us).

Figure 2.19 University of Barcelona (www.ub.edu).

position, that is, at the end of the introductory text for faculties, departments, campuses and parks.

Providing users with cues so that they can discriminate between the links that take them to more content or another page of the same Website that they are visiting (internal link) from those that take them to different pages (external links) is an important recommendation (Nall, Koyani, & Lafond,

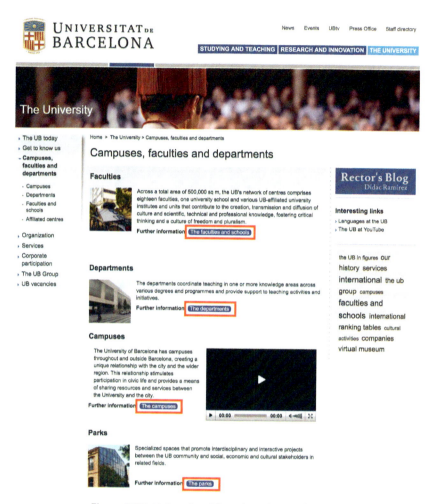

Figure 2.20 University of Barcelona (www.ub.edu).

2001; Nielsen & Tahir, 2002; Spool et al., 1997, among others). In the case of external links, the address of the new Website or the logo of the external institution is usually included to show the user that it is not an internal content of the page they are currently visiting. An example of this strategy can be found at the bottom of the page of The Next Web (see Fig. 2.21). Here we see how the official logos of the social networks (Facebook, Twitter, Google +, LinkedIn, YouTube, Instagram & Pinterest) are included in the literal of the link to show that their respective pages are external and that they do not belong to the Website.

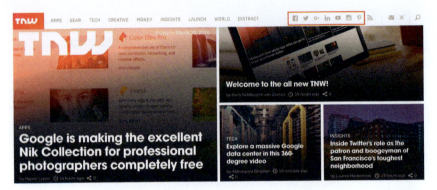

Figure 2.21 The Next Web (www.thenextweb.com).

Another good recommendation is to use contextual links in the form of content lists to reduce the length of excessively long pages. With this resource, if users want to examine all the content of the page, they do not have to scroll down to the bottom of the page (Bieber, 1997; Farkas & Farkas, 2000; Haas & Grams, 1998; Levine, 1996; Nall, Koyani, & Lafond, 2001; Piolat, Roussey, & Thunin, 1998; Schwarz, Beldie, & Pastoor, 1983; Spool et al., 1997; Spyridakis, 2000; Williams, 2000; Zaphiris, 2000; Zimmerman, Slater, & Kendall, 2001). An example of this resource can be found on the page listing the titles of the doctoral programs of the Pompeu Fabra University (Fig. 2.22), where, to reduce the size of the page in question, the titles appear as contextual links that lead the user to other content where these programs are described in greater detail.

Similarly, it is advisable to design the content of the page so that the user does not need to use the horizontal scroll to access all the content it contains. For this reason, Websites are currently designed with a liquid format, adaptable to the display window, so that all the content fits on the screen (Bernard & Larsen, 2001; Lynch & Horton, 2009; Nielsen & Tahir, 2002; Spyridakis, 2000; Williams, 2000).

Finally, to design a good contextual navigation system, it should be remembered that, in the case of internal links, it is important to assign them a semantically informative URL about the linked content. This strategy will improve the position of this webpage content in the results of the search engines.

2.3.1.4 Heuristics for Embedded Systems

Throughout this section we have made a number of recommendations to ensure the correct and independent implementation of each of the different

Figure 2.22 Pompeu Fabra University (www.upf.edu).

embedded navigation system types (constant, local and contextual). Below, and to finish, we offer some recommendations that might be adopted for the integrated and coordinated design of all three system types.

The first recommendation is really quite obvious. Each of these three types of embedded system has to be designed bearing in mind that the ultimate goal is to link them together. This correct articulation should ensure a final Website in which a user is guaranteed flexibility of movement but without feeling overwhelmed by the number of different options.

Another important recommendation is to design the Website in such a way that the three systems do not occupy most of the surface of the page visited. We should not overlook the fact that the ultimate goal of a webpage is communication, and we cannot, therefore, use up all the space on a page with tools for locating information; we also have to provide the user with information.

Moreover, it is interesting to display the content of the labels used in these navigation systems when the mouse is passed over them (employing what is known as 'rollover navigation').

A further recommendation would be to use images or icons instead of linguistic terms in navigation bars. The use of this type of iconic label ensures a more attractive design, albeit one that is also more expensive. If we opt for this strategy, it should not be forgotten that problems of compression for users

Figure 2.23 The Verge (www.theverge.com).

in general may emerge, as well as problems of accessibility for users with some type of visual impairment. One possible solution for overcoming these problems is to include text labels with these iconic labels to clarify the content and facilitate user accessibility, or to use the 'Alt' command key to program the possibility of the label appearing in text form. An example of this first solution can be found on the homepage of The Verge (see Fig. 2.23), where we see how the local navigation system combines iconic labels with text labels.

It is also important to locate the constant and local systems of navigation consistently and in a fixed, clearly differentiated way (Badre, 2002; Bailey, 2000; Bernard, 2001, 2002; Byrne et al., 1999; Detweiler & Omanson, 1996; Ehret, 2002; Evans, 1998; Farkas & Farkas, 2000; Hornof & Halverson, 2003; Koyani & Nall, 1999; Lynch & Horton, 2009; Nielsen & Tahir, 2002; Niemela & Saarinen, 2000; among others). So that the user becomes familiar with these systems, efforts should be made to put them always in the same fixed location within each page of the Website.

Finally, when designing them, we need to be aware, as we have pointed out, that each of these three types of system responds to specific questions, and, therefore, each provides the user with specific information. Thus, constant navigation systems indicate where we are and where we can go; local navigation systems, in contrast, show us what's near the visited page as well as where we can go next; and finally, contextual navigation systems help us identify what is related with what appears in a given content (Morville, Rosenfeld, & Arango, 2015).

2.3.2 Supplementary Navigation Systems

Unlike embedded systems, supplementary navigation systems are information locating resources that do not form part of the actual structure of the Website pages. They are usually independent pages within the site itself. They provide a complementary path for finding new content and implementing tasks via the use of the webpage.

Normally, although not in all cases, they can be understood as a kind of band-aid or solution for overcoming the limitations embedded navigation systems present with respect to the location options. However, if we analyze them in depth, we see that what they are really is an alternative to embedded systems for locating information.

These navigation systems offer two primary basic functions. First, they allow users to orientate themselves as they seek to locate the contents that interest them and as they perform the tasks that can be implemented using the web. The site map is an example of this kind of system that provides orientation. Second, they improve direct access by offering the user a series of shortcuts for finding useful information on the Website. The index is an example of a supplementary system that provides direct access.

The main supplementary navigation systems to be found on a webpage are site maps, indexes and guides.

2.3.2.1 Site Maps

Most books and magazines usually have a table of contents outlining the hierarchy of the information they contain. The table of contents illustrates the structure and the interrelation of the components of the publication (chiefly, its chapters and sections), indicating the physical limits of each of them (the page numbers where they begin and end).

In the same way, the map of a Website provides the user with an overview of the webpage structure. But it also allows the user to navigate within this Website, highlighting the structure of the contents that make it up and providing the user with direct access to that content. To promote this navigation and facilitate this access, sites typically use text or iconic links.

By way of example, Fig. 2.24 shows the site map of the pages of Pompeu Fabra University, outlining the structure and hierarchy of the content that makes up its webpages.

Many studies vouch for its use as an option for user orientation and for facilitating the location of information on pages that include a lot of content (Ashworth & Hamilton, 1997; Billingsley, 1982; Detweiler & Omanson, 1996; Dias & Sousa, 1997; Farkas & Farkas, 2000; Farris, Jones, & Elgin,

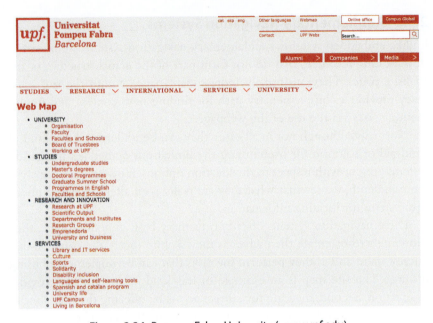

Figure 2.24 Pompeu Fabra University (www.upf.edu).

2001; Kandogan & Shneiderman, 1997; Kim & Hirtle, 1995; McDonald & Stevenson, 1998; McEneaney, 2001; Nielsen, 1996, 1997, 1999a, 1999b, 1999c; Stanton, Taylor & Tweedie, 1992; Tullis, 2001; Utting & Yankelovich, 1989, among others). Moreover, site maps, in XML format, are a tool that not only helps to orientate users but also to orientate search engine crawlers, ensuring that the Website is correctly indexed and that it can be adequately crawled by spiders.

2.3.2.2 Indexes

The index of a Website is a page (included in the same Website) that presents the indexes or the terms that represent the site content, depending on the characteristics and background of the users. Fig. 2.25 shows, by way of example, the index of the EHEA bachelor's degree courses offered by the University of Barcelona.

These indexes are usually presented in alphabetical order, without showing the informational hierarchy between the content, although some pages often display one or two levels of hierarchical depth. It is usually a page that is hierarchically separate from the rest of the pages that make up the site and, by means of links, direct access can be gained to the indexed contents. Thus, it facilitates a much more granular and detailed location of information than that provided by maps.

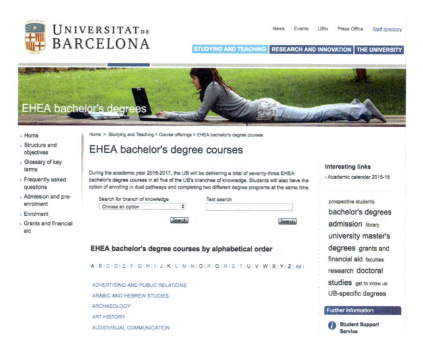

Figure 2.25 University of Barcelona (www.ub.edu).

There are two alternatives for creating an index. If the Website we want to represent with this index is small, this can be done manually by indexing its content and pages. If, however, the Website is much larger, it is best to design a controlled vocabulary and then use automatic indexing software to represent the content and build the index.

2.3.2.3 Guides

Guides constitute a series of tools designed to introduce new users to the content and functionality of a specific part (or subset) of a Website. Unlike maps and indexes that do so for the entire site, guides only provide users with orientation and access to a specific part of the site.

The functionality of guides has been the object of many specialized studies (including Covi & Ackerman, 1995; Morrell, Dailey, Feldman, Mayhorn, & Echt, 2002; Nall, Koyani, & Lafond, 2001; Plaisant, Marchionini, Bruns, Komlodi, & Campbell, 1997, among others). Among these functions, the previous studies stress the fact that guides usually offer the user a contextualization of content. Additionally, guides tend to be based on a linear or sequential search system between content that is linked by an action that the user has to implement.

Guides can be presented in the following formats: as guided tours, as tutorials, as microportals, as tasks or forms. By way of example, the page of the *Wall Street Journal* offers a guide that explains to the user what each of the sections that make up the newspaper consists of, how to navigate them and how to explore them (http://www.wsj.com/guidedtour).

Supplementary navigation systems of this type are usually implemented when first introducing a new task for users to perform on the Website or when users have to undertake a critical task on the webpage and it is important to ensure that they do it correctly. For example, it should come as no surprise to find these resources implemented on pages dedicated to e-commerce (where the critical operation is selling).

As is the case with other architectural structures, there is no set of rules or standardized steps accepted by professionals that can be applied in any context to implement a guide correctly. Yet, despite this, it is possible to offer some recommendations for the design of this type of navigation system.

The first recommendation concerns the size of the guide. Here, to facilitate user orientation, the guides should be short. Moreover, at each step or action that makes up a guide, the user should be able to exit the guide. Likewise, it should not be forgotten that the guide has to be designed to solve problems and, therefore, should incorporate a document or page offering additional information or user support.

In the event that the guide includes tasks, another important recommendation is to standardize these tasks and ensure that the Website server performs the maximum possible number of automatable tasks. As far as standardization is concerned, the navigation tools of guides should always be the same and located in the same position wherever they appear (Bovair, Kieras, & Polson, 1990; Czaja & Sharit, 1997; Detweiler & Omanson, 1996; Foltz, Davies, Polson, & Kieras, 1988; Kieras, 1997; Polson and Kieras, 1985; Polson, Bovair, & Kieras, 1987; Polson, Muncher, & Engelback, 1986; Smith, Bubb-Lewis, & Suh, 2000; Sonderegger, Manning, Souza, Goldman, & Dalton, 1999; Ziegler, Hoppe, & Fähnrich, 1986, among others). In the case of automation, only those tasks requiring intellectual decisions should be reserved for the user (Gerhardt-Powals, 1996; Moray & Butler, 2000; Sheridan, 1997, among others).

It is also useful to include a summary or table of contents if the guide includes many pages and to keep users regularly updated about their progress in completing the task, informing them where they are and what remains to be done (Bouch, Kuchinsky, & Bhatti, 2000; Meyer, Shinar, & Leiser, 1997; Smith & Mosier, 1986).

To facilitate user orientation, it is also advisable to clearly indicate all required fields, limit navigation options, provide users with the possibility of backtracking in the guide to change any previously entered information and allow successive steps in the guide to be recorded so as not to lose the information entered or the actions taken.

Finally, the guides should integrate confirmation strategies to alert users to those actions that, once performed, make the process irreversible, and a system of warnings in which a series of messages alert the user to the possibility of making some kind of error or performing an incorrect action (Lidwell, Holden, & Butler, 2003). An example of such a warning system can be found on the browser when it alerts us to the fact that the Website we are about to visit is unsafe and it warns of the potential risks we run if we access it.

2.3.3 Advanced Navigation Systems

Once the basic navigation systems (embedded and supplementary) have been designed, the advanced navigation models have to be implemented to facilitate the search processes within a Website.

Unlike the basic systems that are included on most of the pages that can be accessed via the network, advanced navigation systems are nonbasic navigation systems that are typically implemented in a small set of Websites.

The main types of advanced navigation systems that can be found on a Website are personalization systems, visual navigation systems and social navigation systems.

Personalization systems are structures that form part of the information architecture of a webpage and that have been designed specifically to reflect user behaviour, needs and preferences.

Personalization systems are proactive navigation structures, which are designed in accordance with user expectations, and which as a result offer the labels and links a user of a given profile will use.

An example of this type of system can be found on the intranet of the University of Barcelona (Fig. 2.26). If users are logged on the intranet, the system remembers their user profile regarding the courses they are enrolled in, their matriculation management, the medical and sports services they use, and the library resources to which they have access.

Visual navigation systems are architectural structures that allow a webpage to be explored using iconic or visual resources. They are usually implemented on pages aimed at children, but they might also be used with adults if what is sought is to exploit the communicative effect of the image. An example of this type of navigation system can be found on the page of the audiovisual

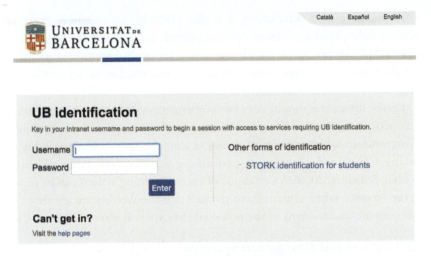

Figure 2.26 University of Barcelona (www.ub.edu).

production company Salt Films (www.saltfilms.com.sg), where all the navigation options are channelled through a hand that is moved with the cursor and that uses interaction with variously shaped salt cellars to access its content.

Finally, social navigation systems are architectural structures for webpage browsing that automatically infer a navigation system by observing the informational behaviour of the majority of its webpage users.

An example of this type of navigation system can be found in the section headed 'Most Popular' in the *New York Times* (http://www.nytimes.com/most-popular). This page incorporates various navigation systems built, among other criteria, by identifying the articles most frequently emailed by readers, linked to in blogs and searched for by the page's users.

2.4 SEMANTIC NAVIGATION

Modern content management systems (CMSs), of which WordPress is a well-known example, use databases to manage information. What might appear to be a simple technicality has had such important consequences that it has marked a before and after in the nature of Websites in one of the most far-reaching, yet, at the same time, one of the most anonymous transformations of recent years.

In a CMS, information is stored in a database, which means the pages are built dynamically every time there is a request for information to the server, rather than being statically stored as in the original web publishing systems.

This clearly adds various layers of complexity to the entire server management process, since it now involves, at least, the information database, a program that manages the requests to the database and that combines the results with one or more style sheets and other elements of semantic organization. It is these that interest us here and that we describe next.

As we have seen, any Website of average complexity usually employs different types of navigation. The main ones (or at least the most visible) are the embedded or primary systems. Some sites, in particular the content-rich sites, usually also have a semantic navigation search system. This system is very important for these sites because it serves to relate the content with other information.

A semantic search system is implemented using both conceptual and instrumental tools. The main conceptual tools are a taxonomy for categorizing a site's content and a semantic search layer based on related topics, while the main instrumental tools are a CMS to manage tags and categories and to identify topics related to the site's content.

2.4.1 Taxonomies

A taxonomy is a term used to refer to a system of classification that presents some kind of structure; in other words, it should be more than a simple list of keywords, while the list should obey some recognizable logical criteria.

As such, a set of topics or subtopics can constitute a taxonomy, but the expectation is that their classes and subclasses (or their categories and subcategories) satisfy the logical criteria as well as they possibly can.

In addition to categories, another of the main tools of content characterization is keywords. We are all familiar with keywords thanks to tag clouds on Websites and Twitter's hashtags. Keywords are also used in all kinds of document databases, for example, in IMDb, in library catalogues to represent (or, more technically, index) documents and in digital media archives. Google also uses them to represent the content of the webpages in their indexes. From all this we can deduce that a taxonomy or classification system is typically associated with categories (classes and subclasses) and tags (keywords).

2.4.2 Menus, Categories and Tags

A content-rich site can have a main menu with, for example, 10 main categories and a further 10 subcategories for each of its main categories. In theory this is more than enough to support a usable navigation system. Naturally there is nothing forcing the site developer to stick to this number; any other number of categories and subcategories, as long as it does not diverge too far from this benchmark, is equally valid for the main menu.

Nor does the site have to be restricted to two levels, although it is not a good idea to add too much depth. Perhaps three and even four are valid, but probably no more. More often than not these components in the main menu correspond in whole or in part to the categories of the site's taxonomy.

Tags, by their very nature, should be much more numerous than the classes that make up the categories. While a category (and even a subcategory) is a 'major class', a tag is the property of each content. Content can be assigned to few categories but can be associated with many tags to ensure this content is represented adequately.

Categories are used to break up the Website in large sections and so they often form part of its main menu. Thus, a newspaper Website will have such sections as Sports, International News and Culture. In this way elements are assigned to a class, while the tags represent the semantic properties of each individual content with as many tags as are required: categories are coarse-grained; tags are fine-grained. Categories contribute elements to the navigation; tags contribute elements to the information retrieval operations.

2.4.3 Distribution of Functions

From a pragmatic point of view, and assuming that the site has managed to establish its main set of categories – essential to begin posting or organizing its content – the distribution of tasks between categories and tags for each site document is structured via an assignment, a representation and a result.

First, the content has to be assigned to at least one category, and possibly to one or two more related categories, but not to many more than that. An article commenting on the latest monetary policy decision taken by the European Bank may be assigned to the Economics category and, perhaps, to that of International News. Then the article is represented with as many tags as considered necessary, including place names and proper names. The same content, however, may be represented with such tags as 'euro', 'Europe', 'currency', 'economy', 'recovery', 'crisis' and 'European Union'. Finally, a result is obtained: typically the document will be assigned to a highly limited number of categories representing the fact that it belongs to very few classes, but it will have as many tags as needed to faithfully represent its semantic content.

It is quite common for the classification system to be controlled, that is, there is a predetermined taxonomy for assigning the content. It would be quite illogical to improvise new categories for each content, although they should be reviewed periodically. When undertaking these reviews, some categories might be modified, some eliminated (and their content assigned to a different category) and new ones added. But it is not an activity that should be carried out daily.

In the case of tags, it is normal practice to combine controlled and free language. Thus, we might start with a set of standard (or controlled) tags but then add tags depending on the input or content, without expecting to find the word already assigned. Note, we speak of 'normal', not obligatory practice. Media publications with a long-standing history use controlled and predefined languages in addition to categories such as tags. More recent media publications with fewer resources tend to build on the fly.

This said, even on sites that use free tags it is often a good idea to periodically review the tags, combining them as far as possible and, of course, reusing them – in other words, checking to see whether we already have a term to express a concept before using a new one.

As we have seen, navigation is based on links. In the case of newspaper sites, the links that facilitate this navigation can be of two types: to other articles or sections of the same medium or to offsite sources and resources.

Both are semantic but from the point of view of SEO they have very different meanings. The former help lower the bounce rate by distributing the PageRank between the site's sections and improving its navigation. The latter in fact are a paradox as they invite the user to exit the site, but in compensation they add credibility to the news story and help search engines understand the relationship between our site and other sites of quality.

In addition, these semantic links can also be presented in two ways: as links embedded in the body of the content or text, and as a separate section, albeit attached to the content. Recall that hypertext links have a starting point, known as the anchor, and a destination, known as the hypertext reference (the href of the source code for a link).

This gives us a faceted typology of semantic links that can be found in content-intensive sites. On the one hand, according to their hypertext reference or destination, we can distinguish between links whose destination is a section or input of the same site and links whose destination is a webpage or section on another site. On the other hand, according to their starting point or location, we can distinguish between links whose anchor is embedded in the body of the entry and links whose anchor link is presented as a list of references attached to the input but separate from its body.

Finally, note that the categories can form part of the constant navigation system on the main page and across the site, of the secondary or lateral navigation on the main page and of the semantic navigation embedded in the individual entries. The tags, on the other hand, can participate as an element in the tag cloud on the homepage, in the semantic navigation in every single content, in the navigation embedded in each individual content and in the keywords for the system of information representation and retrieval.

2.5 NAVIGATION FOR MOBILE DEVICES

A chapter devoted to the subject of navigation would be incomplete if it did not also address this phenomenon in the context of mobile devices (smartphones, tablets, and laptop hybrids).

As we have seen, navigation on large screens typically uses a system of general or primary exploration located horizontally in the upper part of the screen complemented by a secondary navigation system located as a column to the right or that unfolds directly over this upper area and another transversal system that supports hypertext navigation.

However, in the case of mobile devices, such a distribution in many cases is not possible. The inherent characteristics of mobile devices hinder the direct application of versions of the navigation systems used in desktop browsers. The size of their screens and gestural techniques used to interact with them largely impede the unadapted deployment of these navigation systems and so alternative navigation strategies are required.

Specifically, our touch interaction with a mobile device is achieved mainly through 10 basic gestures that substitute the movements we make with the mouse on a nonmobile device: tap, double tap, drag, flick, pinch, spread, press and tap, press and drag, and rotate. The fact that it is our clumsy fingers that implement these actions on a small mobile screen prevents us from comfortably using desktop navigation systems that have been designed to be used with the precise click of a small pointer.

Faced with the impossibility of using those desktop systems, mobile devices have to incorporate other systems or alternative browsing patterns to explore adequately the content they house or the content that is accessed via their wireless connections.

To address these patterns, and based on their specific use, we can classify mobile navigation systems into two groups: systems used for navigating web content and navigation systems that incorporate the applications (apps) of their own devices to facilitate their use.

2.5.1 Web Navigation

Mobile devices usually access the contents of a Website in four different ways: through the original web, using a mobile web, displaying one of the options arising from the responsive web design or using a native mobile application or app.

The first option involves accessing the content of a specific webpage via its original URL without the page suffering hardly any visual changes – in other words, reproducing the same web that can be obtained using a desktop browser but on a smaller scale (adjusting small details like the size of the photographs and typography, for example). The Website of the Pompeu Fabra University (Figs. 2.27 and 2.28) is a good example of a site that

Figure 2.27 Pompeu Fabra University's Website (www.upf.edu) as visited via a desktop browser.

Figure 2.28 Pompeu Fabra University's Website (www.upf.edu) as visited via a mobile browser.

behaves in this way, offering only one, albeit smaller, version, with hardly any changes, when visited from a mobile device.

Offering the same visual version regardless of the type of device (computer or mobile) used to access a webpage may simply be a reflection of financial constraints. Operating a single URL lowers the costs of creating and maintaining a Website. But the consequences for navigation in the case of the mobile device are disastrous. Navigation systems designed for access from a computer become extremely small on the screen of a mobile and require the user to be continuously taking actions, such as increasing the size of the display or scrolling, if the user wants to use it successfully.

The second option is found when the Website offers a visually different version (with a different URL) when it detects that it is being browsed via a mobile device. This version, which is visually distinct from the version offered when accessed via a desktop browser, remains the same regardless of the mobile device (tablet, smartphone or laptop hybrid) used to access it. These versions include various changes, including a new simpler navigation system to facilitate the browsing of the site.

The Website of the *New York Times* (www.nytimes.com and mobile. nytimes.com) is an example of web that behaves in this way, offering a different version depending on whether it is accessed via a desktop browser or via a mobile device.

The mobile web has a number of advantages over the previous option: the Website loads more quickly (given that it offers an architecturally simplified version), facilitates browsing and is better positioned in the results of local searches from a mobile. In terms of its drawbacks, mention should be made of the fact that this option requires building and maintaining (even with regard to SEO) two different versions of the same webpage. Likewise, users have to remember two different URLs if they want to access the page from both types of device. Finally, it should be borne in mind that this option offers the same visual version of the page for all mobile devices from which it is accessed, which might mean it can be visualized and comfortably browsed from a tablet, but the browsing experience might not be as satisfactory from a smartphone.

Responsive web design has emerged as an alternative to original web and mobile web options. In this case, the site uses a single webpage in HTML code, but with the ability to adapt to the screen size of the different devices from which it is accessed. This adaptation is defined by different screen-cut sizes introduced in the CSS code. The page identifies the screen size of the device and provides the web version corresponding to the correct screen cut. In this strategy, the content, design and methods of interaction are adapted to the specific screen size detected. In the case of browser systems, the traditional patterns of distribution of the menus change and focus on the ergonomics applicable to the different screen sizes of the devices from which they are explored. It is not only a matter of changing the width of the page but in defining the functionalities of the site according to the device. On the Internet, for example, at https://bradfrost.github. io/this-is-responsive/patterns.html we can find a myriad of proposals for patterns and modules for responsive designs.

To test whether a webpage has a responsive design, there are several online services that validate the use of a URL on different screen sizes. They include mattkersley (http://mattkersley.com/responsive) and responsinator (http://www.responsinator.com).

The Website of The Next Web is an example of this very strategy. In Fig. 2.29 we can see how the architectural structure of the page changes depending on the type of device it is accessed from. Among the features that undergo adaptation we should highlight the way in which the navigation system is restructured so as to be able to offer all its options regardless of the size of the screen from which it is accessed.

We can trace the history of responsive design back to 2005 when the W3C published the document 'Scope of Mobile Web Best Practices' (W3C, 2005), in which the consortium sought to raise awareness about user experiences in the face of the boom in mobile devices of different sizes. Within that document, the W3C speaks for the first time of 'One Web', a concept that would later lead to the birth of responsive web design. Later, in 2008, the same body published the article 'Mobile Web Best Practices' (W3C, 2008),

Figure 2.29 The Next Web (www.thenextweb.com) webpage as visited from different devices.

thus formalizing its recommendations for mobile web platforms. Here again, in a section dedicated to 'One Web', they call on designers to avoid the creation of multiple platforms for each mobile device. Later, in 2010 Ethan Marcotte, the respected web designer and developer, coined the term *responsive web design* (Marcotte, 2010). The term was nothing more than a play on words that alluded to a new architectural style, and which he believed represented the path that web design should take in facing the multiplicity of mobile devices.

Responsive web design presents a number of interesting advantages. First, the user only has to administer a single webpage and a single URL for all devices, thus reducing maintenance costs and guaranteeing direct access from mobile devices, without having to wait for redirects, which is especially useful when connections are slow. And, second, there is no need to create specific content for mobile devices, as mobile devices continue to enjoy the benefits of the SEO of the desktop web.

But responsive web design also has its limitations. When first launched in 2011, it presented a degree of incompatibility with older browsers, and media queries and page loading with this option were too heavy for mobile phones. Today, with the evolution undergone by browsers and the adoption of broadband mobile browsing, these initial problems have dissipated. Some authors have questioned on more than one occasion the concept of responsive web design, especially as applied to Websites with navigation systems that have deep hierarchies, with categories and subcategories that are burdensome to use from mobile platforms (Budiu & Nielsen, 2012). It has been emphasized that mobile devices have a number of distinguishing features with respect to desktop devices, so the sites require specially tailored differentiated navigation systems. The browsing experience on mobile devices is completely different to that of the desktop, so having only one page, even if it is responsive, can be detrimental to the user experience on both platforms.

Apps (or applications) are the latest option for accessing the Internet from a mobile device. An app is a software application installed on mobile devices or tablets to help the user carry out a particular task. They are usually available via distribution platforms, operated by the companies that own the mobile operating systems, such as Android, iOS, BlackBerry OS and Windows Phone, among others.

The objective of an app is to facilitate the completion of a given task using a mobile device. In the specific case that concerns us here, that task is to access the content hosted on a webpage. But, as we shall see in the next section, an app can also be used to implement any other task from that device.

Many companies have developed apps for mobile devices so that they can access the content hosted on their Websites. The CNN app or that of the BBC are good examples of this type of application.

Generally speaking, apps designed so that a user can interact and navigate with the content of a Website present quite clear navigation patterns, which often reproduce in part the navigation systems of the Website itself, albeit adapted to the size of the device's screen. These patterns are characterized by the vertical presentation of the options on the navigation menu. The vertical distribution pattern facilitates navigation of content regardless of the relationship between the width and length of the mobile screen (wider than it is long in the case of tablets, and longer than it is wide in that of smartphones). The design heuristics recommend that no more than five options be included on navigation menus of this kind. This recommendation avoids the need to use the scroll to browse the system and offers a shallow navigation, which avoids the visual overlapping of the system and the contents being navigated.

Apps make much better use of mobile technology and its resources. From the perspective of user experience, apps tend to offer higher levels of usability than the previously discussed options as they have been designed on the basis of user tests and studies. They can even work without an Internet connection, making information available at any time quickly and smoothly. Moreover, once installed, the app, with its icon, is embedded in the mobile's applications menu, reinforcing branding and giving greater brand presence to the companies responsible for the Website being accessed. Finally, as some studies show, users prefer to spend more time exploring the same content via its app (89% of the time and about 30 hours per month) than through its mobile web (11% of the time and 4 hours per month) (Nielsen, 2014).

However, designing and implementing an app to access the content of a Website is more expensive than doing so via the original site, creating a mobile web or building a Website using responsive web design. In addition, the budget increases if we want to have an app version for each type of device (smartphone and tablet) and for each of the mobile operating systems.

We finish this section by mentioning the existence of webpages whose content can be accessed from a mobile device by simultaneously using more than one of the options described (normally an app and any one of the other options). An example of this strategy can be found on the Time webpage, whose content can be accessed from a mobile device using both its app and its responsive design web.

In the debate as to which is the best option, there would appear to be no clear winner, as each of the solutions can satisfy different goals. The adaptive web design seems to offer an 'all in one' solution: with relatively little outlay, a web multiplatform can be created and access to all users is guaranteed (via computer and/or a mobile device) without any display and navigation problems. However, opting for this solution might see a company miss out on the opportunity to appear in the mobile operating system market and fail to take advantage of the device's technological resources so that its users might explore its content. It is therefore advisable, if the organization can afford to do so, to use both responsive web design and the native application to obtain a more effective and complete mobile solution that will reach all of the company's target audience.

In terms of implementation, the correct strategy to establish a navigable site effectively from any type of device would be to design the Website thinking first in the mobile version before later expanding its capabilities to complete the full desktop version (Wroblewski, 2009). Having satisfied this goal, the next step would be to design the app for each of the platforms.

2.5.2 Navigation App

As we have seen, some of the apps that we can find in the different operating systems of mobile devices have been designed to browse and access Website content. However, the majority are not designed for Website browsing, rather they have been implemented to allow the user to perform other actions (internal file management, entertainment, communication, financial management, control of data related to sport and health, and the production of documents, among many others) through the device itself. Google Play (which allows the management of other applications on the Android ecosystem) and WhatsApp (which allows communication between users via text, voice and file exchange) are examples of such apps.

This second large group of applications, although they do not explore Website content, also present navigation systems to facilitate the implementation of the tasks for which they were designed.

Many authors have identified a number of design patterns in these navigation systems that are repeated in most apps (Banga, 2014; Fling, 2009;

Primary navigation patterns		Secondary navigation patterns
Persistent patterns	Transient patterns	Page swiping
Springboard	Side drawer	Scrolling tabs
Cards	Toggle menu	Expand/collapse panel
List menu	Pie menu	
Dashboard		
Gallery		
Tab menu		
Skeuomorphic		

Figure 2.30 Typology of navigation patterns for apps.

Koch, 2014; McVicar, 2012; McCallister, 2014; Neil, 2014; Monefa, 2015; Purewal, 2014; Sharpe, 2015, among others), motivated, primarily, by navigation recommendations for developers of apps designed for different mobile operating systems (Android, Apple and Microsoft).

As in the web environments where it is possible to distinguish between different basic navigation systems (embedded systems – constant, local and contextual), in the apps it is possible to identify two different groups of basic navigation or exploration patterns: primary and secondary navigation patterns (Neil, 2014).

Primary patterns allow the user to navigate from the top-level categories to the different categories making up the next sublevel in the navigation hierarchy. In the case of the secondary patterns, they supplement the primary patterns, allowing navigation within a chosen level of the hierarchy (Fig. 2.30).

2.5.2.1 Primary Navigation Patterns

Among the primary patterns of exploration we can distinguish between the persistent patterns of navigation, which appear when the user opens the app, and the transient patterns, which appear when the user makes a gesture or taps the device and which are designed to overcome the limitations of the screen size of mobile devices and to allow users to continue browsing using off-canvas areas.

Among the persistent primary patterns, it is possible to distinguish the springboard, cards, list menu, dashboard, gallery, tab menu and skeuomorphic.

The springboard pattern (also called launchpad or hub and spoke) is the classic persistent pattern of navigation and comprises a landing screen with different options that act as a shuttle into the functionality of the application (Fig. 2.31).

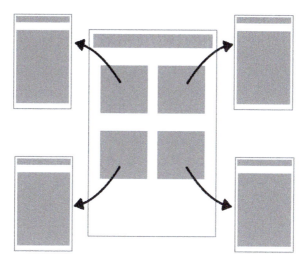

Figure 2.31 Springboard pattern.

It has the same design for all platforms and typically includes up to nine tag options (3 × 3) in the shape of a grid. It is recommended when the primary aim is for the user to see all the functions or tasks offered by the app from the moment it is opened. More menu options can be added by including a paging indicator (ie, dot-dot-dot) at the bottom of the screen. It can be completed by inputting symbols of hierarchy or importance among the categories shown or dynamic information in the titles of the options (eg, number of messages). An example of this navigation pattern can be found in the Vimeo (video management and sharing site) or QR Droid apps (QR code reader) for Android.

The cards pattern is based on the metaphor of a deck of cards and the gestural operations that can be performed using these cards: shuffling, discarding and flipping (Fig. 2.32).

Examples of this navigation pattern can be found in the app supporting Google Now and in the open apps manager for Android (lollipop).

The list menu (or nested doll) is similar to the springboard, but in this case the navigable categories are not presented in a grid but as a list (Fig. 2.33).

Examples of this navigation pattern can be found in the travel app Kayak for iOS and the settings manager of the Android OS (lollipop).

The dashboard is similar to the springboard and list menu patterns. It provides the top-level navigation categories but it brings us bonus information about each of these categories. The pattern provides an interface that includes

Figure 2.32 Cards pattern.

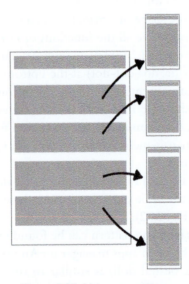

Figure 2.33 List menu pattern.

the console or control panel of the set of tools and indicators of the tasks that can be implemented via the app (Fig. 2.34).

In the Ing Direct France app (Android), we can see how it displays the list of all the banking products that a customer possesses and that the customer can access. But, in addition, it also shows the total balance of the customer's

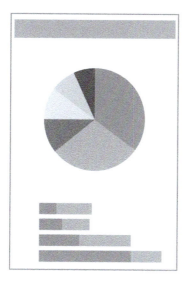

Figure 2.34 Dashboard pattern.

accounts and the quantities associated with each of the products (in numbers and using a bar graph) to avoid the customer having to access them.

The gallery pattern shows live content (typically news stories, recipes and photos) arranged in a grid, a carousel, or a slide show, without there being a significant hierarchy implied in the distribution (Fig. 2.35).

The Instagram app (Android) (and the app for the *New York Times* (Android)) are examples of this type of pattern.

The tab menu (or tabbed view, known as tab bar in iOS) is usually recommended for simply structured apps. In this pattern, a constant navigation system is presented at the bottom (usually) or top of the screen, where it is recommended not to exceed five menu items. The screen presents a collection of sections linked via a toolbar menu that is displayed when the user activates one of the categories (Fig. 2.36).

In the Instagram app we find an example of the tab menu located at the bottom of the display, whereas in the WhatsApp app the menu tab is located at the top. Currently, there is a trend to hide the menu when scrolling down and to make it reappear when scrolling up, and to allow the user to configure the menu or to include text tags to complete the graphic tags and disambiguate them.

Finally, the skeuomorphic pattern is based on an interface design that uses a model or metaphor of something from the real world. This is a trend that means digital designs resemble their nondigital counterparts. Currently

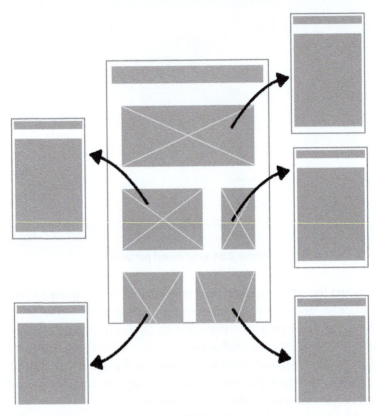

Figure 2.35 Gallery pattern.

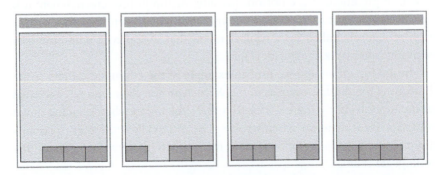

Figure 2.36 Tab menu pattern.

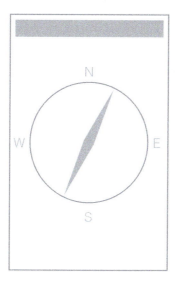

Figure 2.37 Skeuomorphic pattern.

in disuse, the skeuomorphic digital interfaces resemble the real objects that they serve to substitute (Fig. 2.37).

They are found in many applications, especially in entertainment apps (game design, mainly) and in the apps of earlier versions of the iOS for Apple. In the Djay LE app in iOS for mixing music, we find an example of a skeuomorphic interface that emulates a real turntable. In the iBooks app we find, however, an example of skeuomorphics (with wooden shelves and 3D volumes of books) to manage ebooks on a device with an older version of iOS.

Turning to the transient primary navigation patterns, these supplement the primary patterns and allow the user to navigate within the chosen hierarchical level. They are emergent or floating patterns that are hidden from the user until revealed for use and that disappear after use. The main transient patterns are the side drawer, the toggle menu and the pie menu.

The side drawer pattern is a navigation system in the shape of a drawer, which, after tapping the command that activates it (the navicon or the 'hamburger'), can (partially or completely) cover, or move, the original screen in which the command appears (Fig. 2.38).

The toggle menu pattern is a navigation system that also appears on interaction with the device, primarily, by tapping a tag or icon. Unlike the side drawer, the tag or icon presents the navigation categories by theme and they are in turn revealed by a tapping gesture. As in the previous case, this

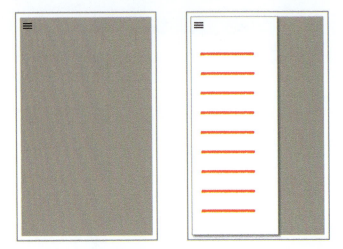

Figure 2.38 Side drawer pattern.

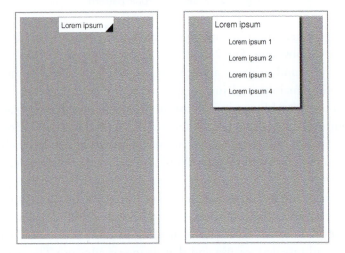

Figure 2.39 Toggle menu pattern.

system may appear as an overlay on the original screen or shift the display to one side (Fig. 2.39).

Finally, the pie menu (also known as wheels, circular menus or radial menus) is a pattern in which the navigation options are presented in an ordered fashion forming a semicircular structure. Normally this pattern is used in entertainment apps (games, primarily), but it can be found in other apps (Fig. 2.40).

Figure 2.40 Pie menu pattern.

The circular navigation system used on the measuring tools app, Multi Measures all-in-one kit for Android, and that used on the settings management app, Pie Control for Android, are examples of such patterns.

Secondary Navigation Patterns

The secondary patterns allow the user to browse the app starting from the categories provided by the primary patterns. In this way the user can continue exploring and using all its features.

Any of the primary navigation patterns can operate as secondary patterns to complete the navigation initiated by the principal system. However, it is also possible to identify a series of patterns that work exclusively in the secondary navigation: page swiping, scrolling tabs and the expand/collapse panel.

In the page swiping pattern users navigate by dragging the different screens that make up the same hierarchical level, while page indicators (normally a horizontal line of dots) inform them of their navigation pattern and let them know which of the possible screens they are viewing (Fig. 2.41).

The scrolling tabs pattern offers a secondary navigating system using tabs to explore the content related with a category from the primary pattern (Fig. 2.42).

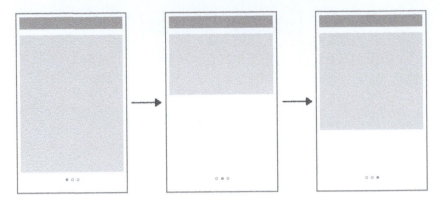

Figure 2.41 Page swiping pattern.

Figure 2.42 Scrolling tabs pattern.

Finally, the expand/collapse panel pattern (or accordion) allows the user to expand or collapse all the content associated with a category in a primary navigation system. It typically uses familiar icons (+, −, > or < symbols) to indicate the expanded or collapsed state associated with a particular navigation category (Fig. 2.43).

Figure 2.43 Expand/collapse panel pattern.

CHAPTER 3

Designing User Experience

3.1 INTRODUCTION

In the last chapter we addressed the conceptual and semantic foundations of navigation and the different patterns and systems (in both web and mobile environments) that enable navigation. In this new chapter, we focus our attention on describing and analyzing methodological questions associated with the implementation of navigation.

Section 3.2 is dedicated to examining the different phases or stages that have to be completed to ensure our navigation resources are designed efficiently. Specifically, we focus on the stages of analysis, design and implementation. The analysis stage examines in detail the scenario in which the site will be developed and includes contextual, content and user analyses. In the design phase, we present the navigation resources and develop content inventory and content models, a representation of the vocabulary, the prototype and an evaluation of the proposed navigation system. Finally, in the implementation phase, an initial version of the navigation system that was drawn up in the design phase is developed, then communicated, before the eventual Website is developed and the style guides created.

Sections 3.3 and 3.4 are dedicated to addressing two of the most frequently used methodological strategies of user analysis, developed to ensure the efficient design of our navigation resources: the Persona and Scenario method and the Card Sorting technique. The Persona and Scenario method is a nonparticipatory analysis technique that seeks both to identify the site's target users and to place their actions within a given context, thus allowing decisions to be taken about the design and structure of our project. The Card Sorting technique is a participatory methodological strategy that allows us to design different (constant and local) navigation systems drawing on the cognitive organizations presented by the site's target users.

3.2 USER-BASED METHODOLOGY

The user has been at the centre of Website development for some time now and is in turn the greatest influence on the development process (Garrett, 2010). The result of this is obvious: today's Website designs are much more

Navigation Design and SEO for Content-Intensive Websites
ISBN 978-0-08-100676-4

Analysis stage	Design stage	Implementation stage
Context analysis	Content inventory	Proposal communication
Content analysis	Content models	Website development
Users analysis	Representation of the vocabulary	Style guides
	Prototype	
	Evaluation	

Figure 3.1 Methodological phases or stages.

useful for users, who, as a result, end up interacting much better with the sites and thus better satisfying their information needs.

So, if we opt for a user-centred design and implementation, this typically means having to follow the series of phases or stages outlined herein: an initial phase of analysis, a second design phase and a third and final phase of implementation.

These three methodological phases or stages, together with their respective operations, are listed in summary form in the table in Fig. 3.1. It should be stressed that we have to implement these operations too for the other structures, especially for the organization and labelling systems that make up a Website's information architecture; and, also, if what we want to do is develop a mobile or native app to access this web content.

3.2.1 Analysis Phase

In the first of the phases, that of analysis (or research), the general scenario in which the web environment is to be deployed, and for which the different navigation resources are to be developed, is studied with precision. A series of critical operations now have to be carried out since failure to do so correctly will condemn the project to almost certain disaster.

There are several reasons why this stage has to be implemented first. One of these reasons is that it allows us to clearly identify what the user really expects of the web that is to be developed. But, also, it allows us to be more effective and efficient (in terms of both time and budget) in the global development of the designs for the navigation resources.

This phase of analysis or research includes a series of operations or studies: a contextual analysis, a content analysis and a user analysis. As Fig. 3.2 shows, each of these analyses in turn includes a number of specific operations (Morville, Rosenfeld, & Arango, 2015).

3.2.1.1 Contextual Analysis

As we have noted, the first step we must take to ensure the success of the design project and the implementation of the Website's navigation system is

Analysis phase		
Context analysis	Content analysis	Users analysis
Background analysis	Heuristic evaluation	Non participatory methods
Presentations and meetings	Content analysis	Participatory methods
Interviews with stakeholders	Content mapping	
	Benchmarking	

Figure 3.2 Operations included in the phase of analysis.

an analysis of the context in which the digital environment will eventually be implemented and used.

To carry out this contextual analysis properly a series of operations have to be undertaken including background research, the planning of presentations and meetings and interviews with stakeholders and internal users.

The background study needs to provide a detailed description of the context and environment in which our digital proposal is to be implemented. We need to begin to determine, for example, what objectives the Website seeks to satisfy, what the overall plan is and, if appropriate, what the accompanying business model is to be, what the audience's characteristics are and what schedule has to be adhered to in its development. This analysis should include the reasons why users will use the web and what it is that will make them come back time and again. We also need to determine what kinds of tasks the users will be able to perform. Moreover, we have to draw up a policy of content provision, determining how this content will be created and managed, and what technical infrastructure model will make this content policy feasible.

Much of this information will be obtained via a series of presentations and meetings, which have to be carefully planned. Here, the goal is to organize a series of introductory presentations to sell the project within the organization and to discuss the Website with some of the people who will eventually be involved in it as content authors, software developers, graphic designers or as marketing experts.

To determine the characteristics of the users of the system under development, surveys or focus group interviews can be conducted, and the marketing studies of the firm for which the site is being developed can be examined.

As we might expect, when the series of operations that make up the contextual analysis are properly implemented, a set of reports should be generated that can serve as a record of the process and that will intervene in the subsequent processes of communication.

3.2.1.2 Content Analysis

Content should be understood as any package of information represented in a document of any format. Hence, a text, audio or video file, an application, or a webpage that forms part of the site can be considered examples of content.

Within environments of this kind, to ensure that users will end up using them and exploiting the information they contain, this content must first be studied. To perform this study or analysis the following operations are usually performed: a heuristic evaluation, content analysis, content mapping and benchmarking.

When our project involves the reformulation of an existing Website, a heuristic evaluation (or expert analysis) can be undertaken by a specialist, who can provide a critical examination of the existing navigation system employing a tried and tested protocol.

Content analysis involves reviewing the contents that will form part of the Website. This review will usually comprise, first, a characterization (examining such dimensions as the format, document type, its source, topic, audience and architectural structure) of a representative sample of the contents or content type and, second, an analysis of the metadata on which to base the information architecture.

Content mapping provides a clear visual representation of some of the results of the heuristic evaluation and of the content analysis. The map shows in a schematic and highly visual form much of the existing information concerning the main content types, indicating the different sources that generate this content, the content models that are generated by each of these sources and the content types that we can find in these models and the architectural patterns that we can find for each type.

Finally, to complete the content analysis it is usual to conduct an exercise in benchmarking. Here, the aim is to identify, evaluate and compare systematically the navigation systems of several websites that are similar to the one we wish to develop, in terms of target audience and objectives, so conclusions can be drawn concerning the best type of navigation for this kind of resource.

3.2.1.3 User Analysis

The users are the eventual targets of our Website and, in this sense, their information needs and behaviour must be seen as being critical for the correct design of the site's navigation system.

However, identifying these needs and behaviour is by no means an easy, straightforward task. Users tend to be complex and unpredictable, especially when it comes to understanding their information behaviour.

There are a number of strategies for studying users, and by drawing on the results they provide, we can undertake a good analysis of user behaviour. As Fig. 3.2 shows, these methodological strategies can be grouped into two broad categories: nonparticipatory methods and participatory methods.

Nonparticipatory methods are strategies for studying user Website behaviour without the users actually knowing that they are being studied. Among the main nonparticipatory methodological strategies we usually find usage statistics software and user behaviour analysis, search–log analyses, mental models, the records from the customer service department and the Persona and Scenario method (which we examine in more detail later).

Participatory methods, in contrast, are strategies for studying user Website behaviour in which the users know they are being studied and where they actively participate in the study. It should be stressed that a suitable sample of the users is first taken and the results are then extended to the entire community of potential users. Among the main participatory methodological strategies we typically find: surveys, focus groups, interviews, the eye-tracking technique, user tests and card sorting (which we discuss later due to its importance in design navigation).

3.2.2 Design Phase

In the design phase, using the information collected in the analysis phase, the navigation resources are decided upon and represented in exhaustive detailed. During this stage content inventory and content models, a representation of the vocabulary, the prototyping and an evaluation of the proposed navigation architecture are usually developed.

3.2.2.1 Content Inventory

Generally speaking, making an inventory of the content is the operation in which all the individual pages and documents making up the Website under development are collected and integrated into the site's architecture.

To draw up the inventory, first, each of the documents (webpages, PDF documents, word documents etc.) that will eventually make up the Website we are designing and developing has to be identified. Once defined, each of the chunks of content is assigned an identification code and a specific destination, that is, a place on the site map. This assignment or mapping is recorded in a document explicitly listing all existing content and its relation with the site pages that have been built using this content.

Finally, an inventory is created (in a spreadsheet or a database, for example), including all existing content and specifying where each content chunk can be found and explicitly describing the hierarchy of these chunks (and so showing the site's global and local navigation systems). The inventory can also describe the possible gaps in the content that will have to be filled in the future by creating new chunks of content.

3.2.2.2 Content Models

Very briefly, the operation for the identification of content models involves the creation of a document that specifies the types of content chunks that make up a Website and the 'microarchitecture' (so to speak) of the information for each type of content chunk. In other words, we are interested in creating a document that specifies the set of elements that make up each type of content chunk and the architectural relationships that exist between them (Morville et al., 2015). Among the functions of a content model, therefore, we find that of supporting the contextual navigation that connects content types and that serves to create hypertext units based on these links, and that of aggregating the linked content.

3.2.2.3 Representation of Vocabularies

To represent the controlled vocabularies involved in our browsing proposal, a document has to be created showing in great detail all the features related with these documental languages. This representation means that later on these information resources can be managed more efficiently.

There are two distinct work products associated with the representation of controlled vocabularies: a metadata matrix and a resource that allows them to be managed. The metadata matrix brings together and specifies the main features of the metadata derived from the vocabularies designed to articulate the Website's information architecture. To ensure the correct management of the terms that make up the vocabulary and the relationships between them, some type of resource, such as a spreadsheet or a database, is typically used.

3.2.2.4 Prototype

Taking into consideration all the information gathered in the content inventory, in the content models and in the representation of the controlled vocabularies, the next step in the design phase is the construction of the prototype that will provide a representation of the navigation proposal. As we shall see in greater detail in the next chapter, this step involves creating and designing a series of diagrams or blueprints that show in both a comprehensive and detailed manner the elements of the information architecture that will structure the Website.

These diagrams or prototypes are designed to serve two essential functions: first, they are designed to represent all the basic features of the navigation resources; and, second, they are designed with the idea of being effective tools for the communication of these basic features of the architectural elements.

3.2.2.5 Evaluation

Before moving into the implementation phase, the architectural proposal for the navigation system has to be evaluated. This involves testing this initial architectural proposal with a sample group of archetypal users of the Website under design. To conduct this test, we might use one of the non-participatory techniques (such as the heuristic evaluation, for example) or, more particularly, one of the participatory methods (for example, card sorting, eye-tracking or, especially, a user test), which we outlined in the analysis phase previously. The latter tests serve to reemphasize the importance of building prototypes that incorporate elements of interactivity and that respect accessibility standards.

Testing our architectural proposal should deliver major benefits. First, it will give us empirical evidence as to whether the design proposal actually meets the requirements identified in the analysis phase. And, second, it will help us to identify potential malfunctions that could have both annoying and costly consequences in the implementation phase. If, as a result of these tests, we discover that our proposal does not meet the requirements identified in the analysis phase or that there are potential malfunctions in the system, then we must introduce the appropriate changes in the proposal and resubmit the new proposal to the same evaluation.

Finally, this design phase should be concluded by drafting a brief and highly visual report summarizing our navigation proposal and showing how this proposal can impact the development of our design project.

3.2.3 Implementation Phase

Finally, in the implementation phase, the navigation proposal, in the shape of the prototype developed in the design phase, is integrated in the final development of the web or mobile environment. This is the stage when, exploiting the outcomes of the previous two phases, the navigation proposal is communicated to all interested parties, the Website is developed and the style guides are created.

3.2.3.1 Communicating the Proposal

Having designed the navigation proposal and taking into consideration the results obtained from the analysis phase, the features of the prototype now have to be communicated to all interested parties.

To ensure that the proposal is incorporated appropriately into the final structure of the web or mobile environment, it is essential to plan a campaign in which the proposal can be presented to the other professionals involved in the site's final development. This presentations phase should be seen as an essential stage before engaging in joint discussions with these professionals. These discussions will enable us to refine, adapt and integrate other functional aspects related to the practical ideas suggested by these professionals into our original architectural proposal. In this process of communicating the proposal, the products obtained in the prototyping operation (blueprints and wireframes), undertaken in the design phase, should be used.

3.2.3.2 Website Development

Having presented and discussed our prototype and adapted our navigation proposal to the requirements of the other professionals involved, we can now proceed to incorporate the resulting proposal within the development or final production of the Website (in HTML). The outcome of this process will be the final version of the environment. This is then ready to be submitted to the necessary final tests or to be presented directly to the end users.

In this operation, various actions are usually performed. For example, a final heuristic evaluation of the navigation system should be carried out on the final version of the environment to detect and eradicate any new errors before its final release. In particular, if the project has involved the restructuring of an existing Website, it is essential to test that all the problems identified in the analysis phase have been eliminated. Also, once the product has been launched, it is advisable to carry out periodic evaluations of the Website to detect new problems and to eventually reactivate the process of navigation development.

3.2.3.3 Style Guides

The final operation in the Website development process is the creation of the style guide for the information architecture of the environment.

The function of this guide is to bring together in one document all aspects related to the information architecture of the environment so that, in the future, those responsible for implementing and maintaining different versions of this environment will continue to respect its initial architectural requirements. As such, the guide serves to ensure that future versions will continue to function correctly from an architectural perspective and maintain their utility for potential users.

3.3 THE PERSONA AND SCENARIO METHOD

All the information collected in the contextual analysis allows us, albeit indirectly, to implement with greater precision one of the most frequently used nonparticipatory methodological strategies for designing Website navigation systems: the Persona and Scenario method.

This is a methodological approach that seeks both to identify the archetypal users or the target audience of our site and to place their actions within a given context, thus allowing decisions to be made about the design and structure of our project.

3.3.1 Persona

The persona method has as its objective the creation and design of all the user types or profiles that make up a Website's target audience so that we, by putting ourselves in the shoes of these archetypal users, can make decisions concerning the user experience of the Website and, in this way, identify the main features to include in the site.

The persona method is a technique used in the design of digital environments, but it is used in many other contexts too, including product development, marketing, communication planning and service design.

It should be stressed at the outset that while the aim is to design profiles that correspond to fictitious characters, the design of these characters is based on all the knowledge we have about our actual target audience (Cooper, 1999; Blomquist & Arvola, 2002). Normally, the method is implemented using information collected by nonparticipatory methods, although it is usually completed with information collected by participatory methods, including surveys and interviews.

Let's imagine that our goal is to design the Website of a new sports newspaper. An example of how a profile of this type might be prepared can be found in Fig. 3.3. The profile describes the principal characteristics of this archetypal user, who we shall call Peter Smith. Specifically, as well as a possible snapshot illustrating Peter Smith's profile, we also include information about what he knows, his tastes, the activities he likes to do, his needs

Peter Smith

72 years old
Retired
Widower
3 children and 6 grandchildren
Lives in Manchester

Skills and knowledge:

Basic training. No university studies
Construction worker all his working life
Low level of information literacy

Likes:

Spending leisure time with his children and grandchildren
Passionate about football. Close follower of all the national football leagues, the England team and English clubs in the Champions League
Reading the daily press
Wants to learn to cook. Loves cooking new recipes
Likes to takes his grandchildren to the cinema once a month

Activities:

Doing the daily housework
Reading the press online each day in the senior citizens' centre
Likes to meet his friends to pay cards in the afternoons in the senior citizens' centre
Picking up his grandchildren when they come out of school

Needs:

To know about the latest film releases and what's on at his local cinemas
To access the press
Would like to be able to do all his administrative paperwork online to avoid having to travel into the city

Limitations:

Barely knows how to use the internet – he has not had nor does he have access to any internet training
Does not have a computer at home or a smart phone with internet access
Needs glasses to read the computer screen

Figure 3.3 Example of profile.

and limitations, etc. As we can see, this profile represents a large proportion of the potential target audience of this new sports newspaper: retired men interested in sports and other forms of entertainment that access the Internet on a daily basis to keep themselves up to date.

Normally, no more than eight archetypal users are identified, but efforts are made to ensure that these personas cover 100% of the site's potential users.

The personas or archetypal users can be either primary- or secondary-type users. In general, the specific web design seeks to satisfy 100% of the needs of the primary users. Specifically, primary archetypal users are those who require their own unique mechanism of interaction, which will not be the case for other personas. This means that if a Website has various primary personas then different information structures and different processes have to be created for each primary persona. Secondary users, in contrast, are those who have needs not contemplated among the principal requirements and so the site will not satisfy 100% of their needs. They are those users who might use an interface designed for another persona. For example, a computer expert might access a recipe Website designed for housewives, but, in general, housewives might not know how to work with an online database. In this case, in the recipe Website, the housewives would be primary personas and the computer expert a secondary persona.

The main advantage of this technique is that it provides a better characterization of the Website's users or target audience than the characterization we obtain when relying on the opinions of a small group of users as recorded in a more participatory method of analysis. To a certain degree, it allows us to use this characterization and the profiles as a control for our architectural proposals. The strategy also allows us to reduce the number of tests of the eventual prototypes that have to be presented to the users, as we can test these prototypes against the profiles generated, without having to interact with users.

However, some authors have criticized the scope of the persona method (Chapman et al., 2006; Chapman & Milham, 2006; Gudjonsdottir & Lindquist, 2008; Rönkkö, Hellman, Kilander, & Dittrich, 2004; Rönkkö, 2005, among others), their main argument being that there is no way of ensuring that the archetypes created are adequate representations of the Website's real users. Other primary and secondary personas could be selected without sufficient grounds to argue that the new outcomes are better than the earlier results. This situation means the persona technique can be criticized for falling some way short of being a true scientific method. The technique has also been called into question for not being able to describe real people, since all it does is represent their characteristics.

3.3.2 Scenarios

In the context in which we are working, a scenario is a description of a persona that pursues a specific goal within a given situation of Website use. In fact, it is a technique that seeks to place the personas in context to see how they behave within that context.

In more technical terms, a scenario is a physical or virtual space in which an archetypal user performs an action, or conversion, using a digital environment to do so. In the context of a Website, a conversion is achieved when one of its users performs an action for which the site was designed (buys something, reads an article, makes a comment or finds information, among other things). This conversion is directly affected by the user's social, work, family and personal conditioning factors and by the features and design of the digital environment. In the same way as personas, scenarios are created from interviews or direct observations of real users. Also note that a scenario can serve different personas, and a persona can act in different scenarios.

Scenarios are typically used to contextualize the personas or archetypal users identified so that we can discuss possible design solutions for the Website development. They can be used at the start of a project to help flesh out requirements or as tools to explore and validate design solutions. They are also often used to compare our design proposals with those of the competition or to test final designs.

Returning to our archetypal user, Peter Smith, the following represents a simple example of the scenarios that might be designed:

'It's 12:00 in the morning, Peter has just gotten home after doing the daily shopping. He's bought some peas and wants to serve them up in a new recipe, to surprise his son who is coming for lunch today. Down at the market, he heard that next week they will be selling a new exotic fruit from Latin America. It's called the *pitahaya*, and they said they would let him try one. He'd like to know what it tastes like. Yesterday, his football team, Manchester United, beat their opponents in the weekly game in the Premier League and he'd like to find out all the details from the press. Pixar's latest film premieres this Friday and he'd like to know in which local cinema it's showing so he can take his grandchildren to see it. The phone rings. It's his financial adviser reminding him that he has to submit his online tax declaration within the next 10 days.'

Three main types of scenarios can be identified. First, there are those that describe high frequency actions. These are the principal scenarios and include very common tasks or conversions. Second, there are scenarios that describe necessary tasks or conversions, which while not frequently performed, have to be implemented every now and again. Third, there are those that describe marginal or largely unusual actions. Some professionals claim that these actions can be ignored, given that addressing them can involve a low return on investment.

In the case described, when Peter is interested in finding out from the press how his football team played and what's on at the cinema this week, these can be considered examples of the first type of scenario, as they describe very common, high frequency, actions. In contrast, his online tax declaration can be considered an example of the second type, describing a necessary, but not very frequent, action. Finally, his curiosity to find out what a *pitahaya* tastes like exemplifies a scenario that describes unusual or marginal tasks.

The main advantage afforded by the scenario method, in combination with that of the persona technique, is to provide a mechanism for exploring design solutions. However, some professionals are critical of the actual scope of this methodology. Mainly, they claim that it is too simple and deceptively empirical, reducing as it does the complexity of reality to that of just a few people and scenarios or to very specific contexts in which attempts are made to solve too many problems simultaneously.

3.4 CARD SORTING

Card sorting is one of the most powerful tools used in Website navigation design; however, it is not normally applied to the development of navigation for apps given the limited number of labels that make up their systems.

Originally, this technique was designed by psychologists to study how people organize and categorize their own knowledge. Generally speaking, in web environments, it is a technique in which a small group of potential site users are asked to sort a set of cards (labels or concepts) that reflect their mental models. In turn, these models then serve as inspiration for architects to structure a Website. Normally, the labels making up the navigation system, or those that comprise the organization system (that is, the labels that we are ultimately interested in organizing), are written on these cards and each card is numbered to facilitate further exploitation. Finally, the users are asked to group the cards by topic and to write (on a Post-it, for example) a category to serve as a name for each group.

The grouping of the cards offers a number of important benefits. For example, we can conduct user tests on the navigation, labelling and organization systems proposed as part of the information architecture; we can extract the tacit organization that users might employ when interacting with the web; and, we can identify the mental models that typify our archetypal user. In short, what we manage to achieve is to define more appropriately (given that the definition is based on the mental constructs of the users themselves) some of the most important features of the navigation system (both constant and local; and the labels that make them up), together with those of the organization, the labelling, and, more indirectly, the search systems.

In the rest of this section, we describe the different types of card sorting that can be implemented depending on what it is we are specifically interested in analyzing and the methodological strategies that need to be carried out to ensure the results are put to good use.

3.4.1 Typology

Depending on the specific criterion adopted, different classifications can be made of the types of card sorting available for use.

Thus, for example, if we take as our criterion the categories for classifying the labels used in the technique, we can distinguish between open- and closed-card sorting. In the open-ended method users are free to group the labels into the number of categories they consider necessary; the only thing they are asked to do is to explain the criteria used in making the groupings. In contrast, in the closed method the categories are predefined and labelled and the users only have to place each label in what they consider to be the most appropriate category. The latter is used particularly to test an existing (constant and local) navigation system.

However, if we take as our criterion the participants involved, we can distinguish between individual and collective card sorting. The individual method involves applying the technique with a single user, whereas the collective method is applied to multiple users and provides us with an average of the group's results.

Again, if we take as our criterion the type of user interaction, we can distinguish between face-to-face and virtual card sorting. In the former, the technique is applied in the physical presence of the user; while in the latter, the user implements the technique remotely, online.

Finally, if we consider the type of application used, we can distinguish between three different types of card sorting: manual, semiautomatic and automatic. In the case of implementing a manual card sorting technique (ie, data collection and their exploitation) no tools or software are used; all that is typically required are a set of cards, a pencil and (usually) a packet of Post-its. In the case of the semiautomatic method, tools or software are also used to collect and exploit the data. There are many tools available to implement this technique. Among the most common, mention should be made, for example, of Optimal Sort, UXsort, CardBoard, UserZoom, SimpleCardsort and xSORT. Finally, in the case of the automatic method, various kinds of tools or software can be used for its implementation (ie, data collection and their exploitation) and for generating the organization and navigation systems derived from it. AutoCardSorter, among others, is a good example of such a tool. This tool allows user data to be collected and exploited and for a Website navigation system to be generated automatically from these data and the outcomes of prior semantic and statistical analyses.

3.4.2 Methodology

Alternative methodologies exist for implementing the card sorting technique. However, four phases are typically needed to complete their implementation correctly: label selection, implementation, analysis and presentation of results.

In the first phase, the labels are selected. Here, more specifically, we should only propose labels that might form part of the eventual local navigation system. In the case of closed-card sorting, the categories of the constant or global system are the ones proposed by the analyst, and the users are required to group the labels in these categories. In the case of the open-ended method, the names of the categories of the constant or global system are obtained after analyzing the proposals made by the users, who provide the names for each set of grouped labels.

It should be stressed that the labels used in the study should be as meaningful and as comprehensive as possible, and they should present the same type of granularity and semantic specificity. There is no consensus on the number of labels that should be subject to study, although usually between 30 and 100 are used. When selecting them, it is important to take into account any possible ambiguity they might cause among the users and to select labels that are free of such problems.

In deciding on the labels, inspiration can be drawn from the navigation systems of competitors' Websites or those with the same target users. For example, if we want to remodel the navigation system of the Website of a daily newspaper, we could obtain labels for our card sorting by the analyzing the local navigation systems of, let's say, *USA Today*, the *New York Times* or the *Washington Post*. Fig. 3.4 shows all the labels resulting from such an analysis.

The implementation phase begins by recruiting participants. Typically between 15 and 30 participants are recruited, respecting the archetypes and their respective proportionality within the target audience as obtained from implementing the Persona and Scenario method. For each participant a brief report is prepared identifying their sociological and demographic profiles. Once the participants have been recruited and analyzed, the technique can be implemented. Here, the participants are usually asked to read a text explaining the technique; and in the case of face-to-face card sorting (with a moderator) a template is usually prepared to facilitate data collection.

In the analysis phase, two types of studies are undertaken: a qualitative analysis and a quantitative analysis. To implement the qualitative analysis a questionnaire is administered to analyze the users and their background and all the information gathered by the moderator of the process is collected. In the quantitative analysis an attempt is made to identify the

		USA	NYT	WP
News	World	Nation	First Draft	Courts & Law
	Nation	World	Inside Congress	The Fed Page (federal)
	Elections		Poll Watch	Polling
	Law	Elections	The Upshot	
Money	Markets	Markets	International	Get there
	Small Business	Business	DealBook	Wonkblog (economía y política doméstica)
	Real State		Markets	
		Personal Finance		Markets
	On Leadership (claves para el liderazgo empresarial)	Cars	Economy	
				Know More
			Energy	Storyline
			Media	World Business
			Technology	Capital Business
			Personal Tech	Digger
			Small Business	On Leadership
			Your Money	On Small Business
			Real State	
Entertainment	People	People	Arts	Books
	Movies	Movies	Style	Comics
	Music	Music	Food	Going Out Guide
	TV	TV	Health	Horoscopes
	Books	Books	Travel	Movies
		Entertain This!	Education	
	Museums	(Celebrities Gossips)		Museums
			Fashion & Style	
	Gossip	Best Selling Books		Music
	Arts	TV Schedule	Health	Puzzles & Games
	Puzzles & Games	Puzzles	Home & Garden	Theater & Dance
	Horoscopes	Games	Jobs	TV
		Horoscopes	Real State	Jobs
LifeStyle	Education		Celebrities	
	Health		Fashion	

Figure 3.4 Labels resulting from the analysis of the navigation systems of the websites of USA Today, the New York Times and the Washington Post.

adequacy/dispersion of a term or label in relation to one or more categories, the relationships between the terms and labels, the consistency of a
category, the relationships between the categories and semantic proxim-
ity/remoteness of the category names (in the open-card sorting).

This quantitative analysis can be illustrated in greater detail using a simple example. The first step in completing the quantitative analysis is to
obtain the numbers or data from the study and to represent them in two
different types of symmetric matrices: the symmetric matrix of absolute
values and the symmetric distance matrix. The two matrices have the same
structure obtained from the Cartesian product of the set of labels multiplied
by itself. In this sense, designing each of these matrices only requires that as
many rows and columns be included as there are labels or terms in the study.

The symmetric matrix of absolute values is a table of data (the Cartesian
product of the set of labels) generated in a spreadsheet showing the number
of times each pair of terms is grouped together, that is, their co-occurrences.
In other words, it shows the number of times the test participants grouped
a term together with another. To illustrate how this first type of matrix
works, imagine that we are undertaking a test with a number of users to
design the navigation system of a newspaper Website in which there are
four labels being studied: 'Football', 'Golf', 'Theatre' and 'Cinema'. Fig. 3.5
shows what the symmetric matrix of absolute data for this example might
look like. As we can see, the terms or labels 'Football' and 'Golf' have been
classified in the same group 17 times, the terms or labels 'Football' and 'Theatre' have never been classified in the same group and the terms or labels
'Theatre' and 'Cinema' have been classified in the same group 12 times.

The symmetric distance matrix shows the distance between two terms,
so that we can determine the proximity between them: the closer they are
to the value 1, the stronger the correlation and the lower the distance
between the two terms; the further they are from the value 1, the weaker
the correlation and the greater the distance between the two terms. If the
distance takes the value 1, then the two terms have been matched by all the

	Football	Golf	Theatre	Cinema
Football		0.739	0	0
Golf	0.739		0.174	0.087
Theatre	0	0.174		0.552
Cinema	0	0.087	0.552	

Figure 3.5 Symmetric matrix of absolute values.

	Football	Golf	Theatre	Cinema
Football		17	0	0
Golf	17		4	2
Theatre	0	4		12
Cinema	0	2	12	

Figure 3.6 Symmetric distance matrix.

users participating in the test. To calculate the distance, x, between two labels, the following formula can be used: $x =$ number of participants who have classified these two labels together divided by the total number of participants in the test. Fig. 3.6 shows what the symmetric distance matrix for this example might look like. As we can see, the terms or labels 'Football' and 'Golf' are very close, at a distance 0.739; the terms or labels 'Theatre' and 'Cinema' are at an intermediate distance (0.522); while the terms or labels 'Football' and 'Theatre' are completely separate (0).

When these symmetric matrices incorporate a large number of data, it is usual to present them in graph form, using a dendrogram, to facilitate interpretation.

The dendrogram is used to show the relationships of proximity or distance between the terms or labels. Fig. 3.7 shows the dendrogram obtained once the users have carried out the card sorting. As we can see, the terms that are closer to one another appear together and are given the same colour to form a set. This means that, according to the users that performed the test, each of these groups of terms or labels could form part, at the same level, of the same branch within the classification and be grouped in the same category.

It should be stressed that the position of the vertical line determines the limit for creating the groups. If we move the position of the line to the left, more groups of labels are formed; or what amounts to the same, our constant navigation system will comprise more categories. If we move the position of the line to the right, fewer groups are formed; or what amounts to the same, our constant navigation system will comprise fewer categories.

The position of the line is one of the decisions that the information architect has to take, based on the implementation of the systems and the architectural structures. However, to establish the number of categories that will make up the constant navigation system, one of the following criteria can be followed. We can study how many categories make up the constant navigation on similar sites and adopt this same number for our system. Or,

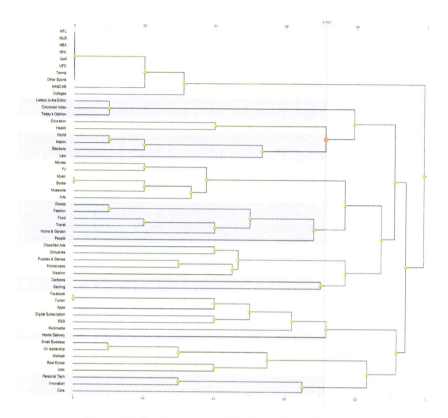

Figure 3.7 Dendrogram resulting from the card sorting.

if this number is not available, we can determine the number of categories by calculating the square root of the total number of labels that will make up the local navigation system (from the complete set of labels used in the card sorting). This will guarantee a balanced navigation in both breadth and depth. In the case of our newspaper Website, we shall opt for a compromise solution of nine categories for the constant navigation system. An examination of similar sites revealed an average of around nine categories (eight in the case of *USA Today*, 17 for the *New York Times* and 13 for the *Washington Post*) while the square root of 57 (total number of labels in the constant navigation system) leads to a proposal of around seven categories.

In addition to the dendrogram, the card sorting tools provide us with the raw data for each user (Fig. 3.8). This means all the information obtained can be stored and consulted at any time when more information is required about the results. Indeed, their use is recommended for a more detailed analysis, but obviously this adds greater complexity to the task.

. **Raw data per participant**

UZ_ID	CAT_1	CAT_2	CAT_3	CAT_4	CAT_5
C475S15...	"Arts", "Columnist Index", "Education", "Elections", "Markets", "Nation", "Weather", "World"	"Facebook", "People", "Twitter"	"Apps", "RSS"	"Digital Subscription", "Home Delivery", "Letters to the Editor"	"Gaming", "Puzzles & Games"
C475S15...	"Cars", "Jobs", "Markets", "On leadership", "Real Estate", "Small Business"	"Colleges", "Golf", "MLB", "NASCAR", "NBA", "NFL", "NHL", "Other Sports", "Tennis", "UFC"	"Apps", "Facebook", "Gaming", "Innovation", "Personal Tech", "Twitter"	"Columnist Index", "Letters to the Editor", "Today's Opinion"	"Fashion", "Gossip", "Home & Garden", "Horoscopes", "Movies", "People"
C475S15...	"Columnist Index", "Elections", "Letters to the Editor", "Nation", "Obituaries", "People", "Today's Opinion", "Weather", "World"	"Colleges", "Education", "Health", "Law"	"Innovation", "Markets", "NASCAR", "On leadership", "Real Estate", "Small Business"	"Apps", "Facebook", "Gaming", "Jobs", "Multimedia", "Personal Tech", "Twitter"	"Arts", "Books", "Cars", "Cartoons", "Fashion", "Food", "Gossip", "Home & Garden", "Home Delivery", "Horoscopes", "Movies", "Museums", "Music", "Puzzles & Games", "Travel", "TV"
C475S15...	"Education", "Food", "Health", "Obituaries", "People"	"Cars", "Cartoons", "Fashion", "Gaming", "Gossip", "Home & Garden", "Puzzles & Games", "Travel"	"Apps", "Classified Ads", "Digital Subscription", "Facebook", "Home Delivery", "Horoscopes", "Jobs", "RSS", "Twitter", "Weather"	"Markets", "On leadership", "Real Estate", "Small Business"	"Elections", "Law"
C475S15...	"Golf", "MLB", "NASCAR", "NBA", "NFL", "NHL", "Other Sports", "Tennis", "UFC"	"Arts", "Education", "Elections", "Health", "Markets", "Nation", "Weather", "World"	"Books", "Cars", "Gaming", "Home & Garden", "Movies", "Multimedia", "Music", "Personal Tech", "Real Estate", "TV"	"Apps", "Classified Ads", "Gossip", "Horoscopes", "Jobs", "Obituaries", "Puzzles & Games"	"Cartoons", "Columnist Index", "Letters to the Editor", "Today's Opinion"

Figure 3.8 Detailed final results of the card sorting.

NEWS ▼	OPINION ▼	SPORTS ▼	FREE TIME ▼	FUN ▼	ECONOMY ▼	TECH ▼	MORE ▼	FOLLOW & SUBSCRIBE ▼
Education	Letters to the editor	NFL	Movies	Cartoons	Small Business	Personal Tech	Classified Ads	Facebook
Health	Columnist index	NHL	TV	Gaming	On leadership	Innovation	Obituaries	Twitter
World	Today's Opinion	MLB	Music		Markets	Cars	Puzzles & Games	Apps
Nation		NBA	Books		Real Estate		Horoscopes	Digital Subscription
Elections		Golf	Museums		Jobs		Weather	RSS
Law		UFC	Arts					Multimedia
		Tennis	Gossip					Home Delivery
		NASCAR	Fashion					
		Colleges	Food					
		Other Sports	Travel					
			Home & Garden					
			People					

Figure 3.9 Constant and local navigation of a newspaper Website.

Having completed the analysis, all that is left is to build or refine the local and constant navigation in the light of the evidence provided by the dendrogram and the users' proposals. In Fig. 3.9, we propose a constant (nine categories) and local navigation system (53 labels) based on the outcomes of our card sorting for the navigation design of a newspaper Website.

CHAPTER 4

Prototyping for Navigation

4.1 INTRODUCTION

As we saw in the previous chapter, the design, planning and implementation of the navigation resources of an information environment – that is, a Website or an app to access this web content, for example – needs to be based on a prototyping proposal for the architectural structure of this information environment.

Prototyping is the graphical representation of the various components of the basic architectural structure that will help guarantee the utility of this Website. In other words, it is concerned with creating and designing a series of diagrams that depict in a detailed and exhaustive manner the architectural elements that structure the Website.

This chapter has two aims: first, to analyze the functions of prototyping and prototyping typologies; and, second, to describe and review a series of online and desktop tools designed to facilitate the creation of prototypes for the design and creation of webpages and digital content for mobile devices.

To meet these goals, the rest of the chapter is organized as follows. In Section 4.2 we begin by outlining the importance and functionality of prototyping for the architectural design of a Website. In Section 4.3, we analyze the two main types of prototypes or diagrams typically used to represent the architecture proposed for a webpage: blueprints and wireframes. Finally, in Section 4.4, we review some of the main (online and desktop) solutions for developing and implementing Website diagramming or prototyping.

4.2 FUNCTIONS OF PROTOTYPING

The appropriate specification of requirements plays a fundamental role in the success of what is, at times, the very complicated process of Website conception and design, especially if the site is to host large volumes of information and/or support complex functions (Hamm, 2014).

In turn, prototyping is a fundamental and critical component of the set of elements that make up the Website specification, since it is directly linked to the conception and development of the site's future information architecture and, more particularly, of its navigability.

Navigation Design and SEO for Content-Intensive Websites
ISBN 978-0-08-100676-4

85

The primary outcome of the prototyping is a series of diagrams. These diagrams or prototypes are designed to meet two basic functions: one representational and the other communicative.

In the case of the first of these functions, the prototypes are designed to represent all the basic features of the Website's architectural elements, expressly avoiding, if so desired, all questions related to graphic design. These features essentially include the components of each of the systems (organization, labelling, navigation, search and controlled vocabularies) that make up the anatomy of the site architecture, the structure of the content that makes up the site and the relationships between them.

As for the second function, the prototypes are designed with the idea that these basic features of the architectural elements can be communicated effectively (Brown, 2010). This second function takes on a very important dimension if we bear in mind that, to ensure the successful completion of the Website design and development project, the information architect's proposal needs to be combined with the contributions of other professionals involved in the project including, for example, designers, developers, content authors, the project managers themselves as well as experts in usability and user-centred designs (McNeil, 2012).

Finally, the proposal has also to be examined and, eventually, approved by the party that is willing to finance the project. Therefore, the prototype also fulfils a strategic function of communication between the design team and those responsible for giving the project the go-ahead or for cancelling it.

To facilitate the design, standardization and communication of the diagramming or prototyping proposals, there are a series of well-established, visual or iconic languages and vocabularies (with their own syntax and semantics) that enable the representation of the architectural features and elements referred to before. Among these languages, one of the best known and most widely used is that suggested by Jesse James Garrett (2010). His language shows a proposal for representing visually most of the elements (pages, files, stacks, areas, and the conditional elements of clusters, branches and selectors, among others) and relationships (connectors and arrows, among others) that make up the architectural structure of a Website (www.jjg.net/ia/visvocab).

4.3 TYPES OF PROTOTYPE

Two main types of diagram or prototype are typically used to represent the architectural proposal for a Website: blueprints and wireframes.

4.3.1 Blueprints

The blueprint (plan or map) of a Website can broadly be understood as a diagram that represents the architectural structure of that Website, showing all its pages and the different relationships between the homepage, the pages that make up the site and the content of these pages.

They are used to highlight the essential features of the organization, labelling and navigation systems. They are often referred to as the 'site map' and they are a key tool in facilitating the further work of the web developers and in orienting the site's users.

Depending on the specific perspective addressed, we can discriminate between two main types of blueprint: blueprints used for the overall architecture (or high-level blueprints) and blueprints used for the detailed architecture (Morville, Rosenfeld, & Arango, 2015).

Blueprints of the overall architecture are usually highly schematic: starting from the home page, the pages that make up the Website, the relationships between these established through the links that connect them and the way in which these are grouped in the organization and navigation systems. They are typically used to discuss the overall site architecture, to demonstrate the Website organization to those responsible for commissioning the site and as a guide for the site's designers and developers and for the users (and later being used to generate the site map). So they can be interpreted correctly, they are normally accompanied by a small legend that explains the meaning of the symbols of the visual language used in their construction. We can see an example of this type of blueprint in Fig. 4.1, which shows an architectural proposal for the creation of an online newspaper site. The lower panel of the figure houses the legend explaining the visual language used.

In contrast, blueprints of the detailed architecture show, for each of the pages that make up a Website, a highly schematic representation of the pages that in turn hang from them and the navigation system that articulates them. They are also typically used to discuss the architectural features related to these pages, as a guide for the site's web designers and developers, and once they are implemented in the functional version of the Website, as a resource for completing the organization and navigation systems and for helping users locate information. In the same way as those used for the overall architecture, to ensure the correct interpretation of these blueprints, they are accompanied by a small legend explaining the meaning of the symbols of the visual language used in their construction. We can see an

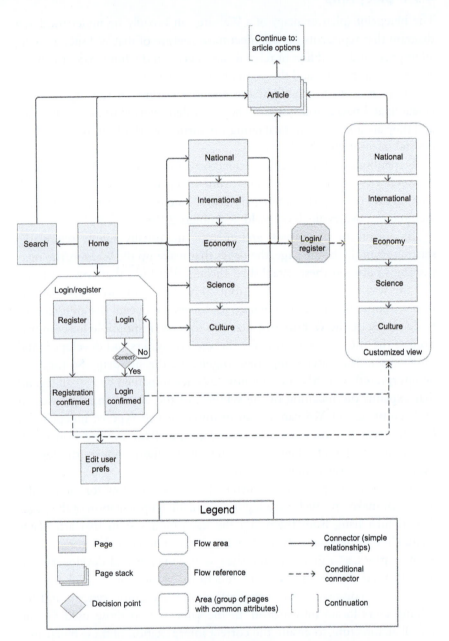

Figure 4.1 Example of a blueprint of the overall architecture.

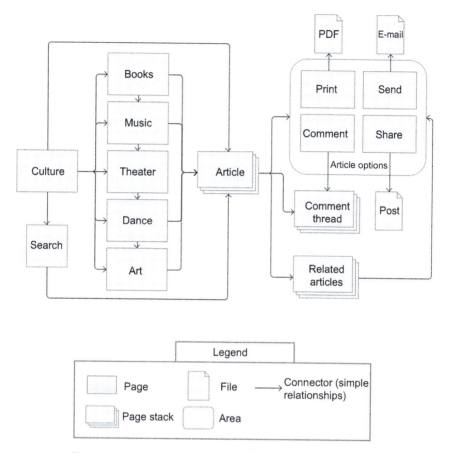

Figure 4.2 Example of a blueprint of the detailed architecture.

example of this type of blueprint in Fig. 4.2, which shows the architecture of a page from the culture section of an online newspaper site. Again, as in the previous figure, the lower panel of the figure houses the explanatory legend of the visual language used.

4.3.2 Wireframes

Wireframes (or mock-ups) are architectural prototypes of each of the page types that make up a Website. They provide a schematic diagram of the content and the information architecture (but without any graphic elements) of each of these page types. As such, they show what each page looks like from the perspective of its architecture, emphasizing how the page components are grouped and ordered. In a way, they can be considered as

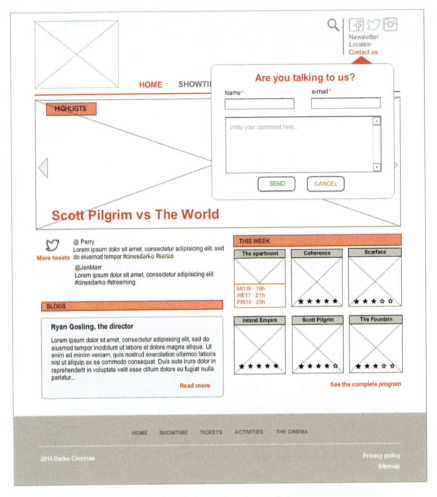

Figure 4.3 Example of a wireframe.

being the intersection between the information architecture and the visualization and design of the page.

An example of a wireframe can be seen in Fig. 4.3. Here, the wireframe provides an architectural proposal for the creation of the homepage of a cinema chain. As we can see, among other elements, the wireframe typically represents the position of the navigation system, the location of the links, the page structure and the location of the search system. Only the features that are relevant from an architectural point of view are represented, which means that all the visual and design features, such as the font type/size used in the text and the background colours used on the page, are left out. It

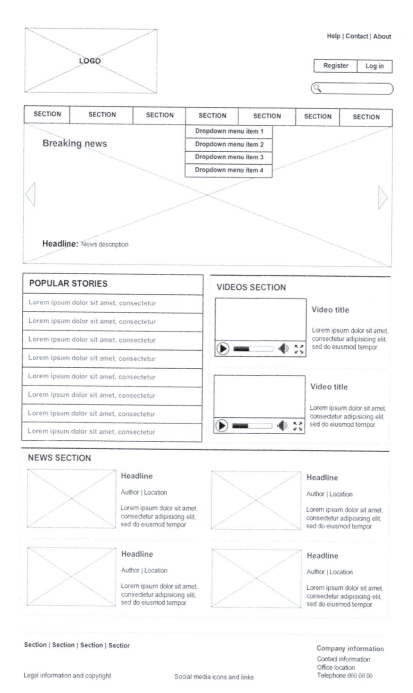

Figure 4.4 Example of a low-fidelity wireframe.

should be stressed that these architectural representations are often used in conjunction with blueprints, so that changes or modifications in one end up producing changes in the other.

Wireframes are usually drawn for most page types making up a Website; although more particularly, a detailed wireframe is developed for the main or homepage, the site's most important pages, pages providing user support or the page housing the search interface.

Like the blueprints, they are typically used to discuss the architecture of the page types and to talk about their architectural features with other professionals (designers, developers and content creators, for example) involved in the design and creation of the Website.

Depending on the granularity they present, typically three types of wireframe can be identified: low-fidelity, medium-fidelity and high-fidelity wireframes (Morville et al., 2015).

Low-fidelity wireframes usually show the basic architectural features of a webpage type, without including graphic elements and without any actual content. In short, they only represent elements of the global, local and contextual navigation of the page. An example of this type of wireframe can be seen in Fig. 4.4, which shows an architectural proposal for the creation of the homepage of an online newspaper Website.

Medium-fidelity wireframes, in contrast, usually present the basic architectural features of a webpage type including some of its graphic elements as well as some units of actual content. In short, they represent elements of the global, local and contextual navigation of the page in conjunction with other definitive elements that will appear in the version of the webpage offered to the user. An example of this type of wireframe, offering an architectural proposal for the creation of the homepage of the online version of a newspaper, can be seen in Fig. 4.5.

Finally, high-fidelity wireframes usually represent the basic architectural features of a webpage type including all the graphic elements and actual content that will complete the page. In short, they represent the elements of global, local and contextual navigation of the page in conjunction with all the definitive elements that will appear in the final version of the webpage that the user can visit. They are usually designed directly in HTML so as to give a more realistic picture of what the Website will eventually look like. An example of this type of wireframe developed for the homepage of a newspaper can be seen in Fig. 4.6.

Compared to the other two wireframes, the advantages of this type of prototype are clear. First, they include many other features (colours, font

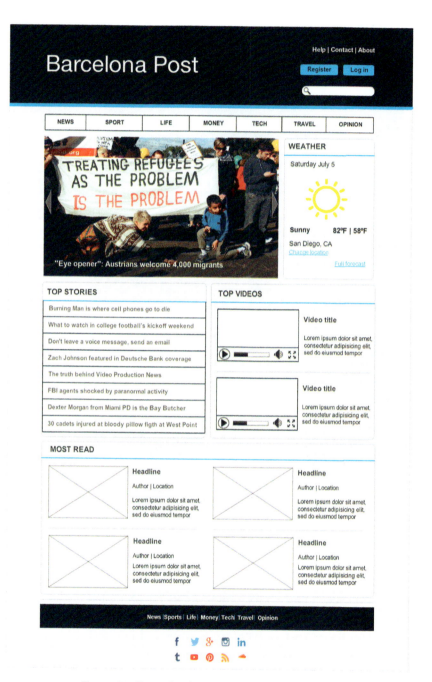

Figure 4.5 Example of a medium-fidelity wireframe.

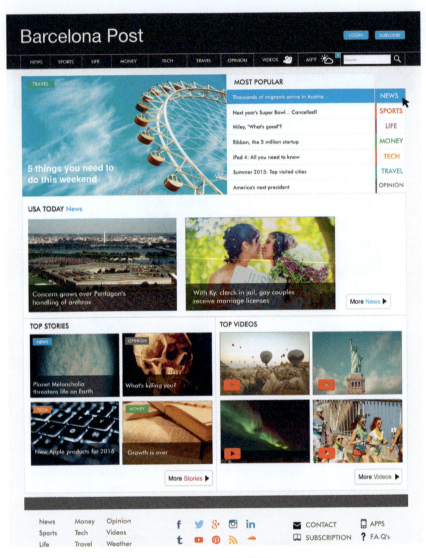

Figure 4.6 Example of a high-fidelity wireframe.

size and type, etc.), beyond the purely architectural, related to the usability of the page. And, second, by including all these features they are better candidates than the other two types to be employed in user tests and in page evaluation, guaranteeing greater benefits. But the development of this type of prototype also presents certain drawbacks. First, its development involves greater effort and costs than the other two types of prototyping. And, second, the fact of generating them with such a high degree of fidelity means having to design the style book and design guides for the whole Website project at a point in the project when all the features of the design, the architecture, usability and accessibility of the pages that comprise it have yet to be selected and decided upon.

Leaving aside the type of wireframes, and although there is no clear methodology for implementing them, it is possible to list, albeit in summary form, a series of recommendations that should be followed to ensure the utility and efficiency of this type of prototyping.

For example, each page type should be consistent and be deployed with the same level of granularity. This uniformity and consistency will avoid subsequent inconsistencies in the work of the developers as they create the webpages.

Second, it is also advisable to decide upon the legends and explanatory notes that will govern the visual language used to build the prototype. These legends and notes will facilitate explanations of the functionality of the page elements and communication of the features of the information architecture to other professionals (designers and content creators, for example) involved in the Website development.

It is highly recommended to implement good control and management measures of a site's wireframes. For example, it is a good idea to assign a name to each wireframe, specify which project it belongs to, indicating the specific number of the version being worked on and its date of creation. These control and management measures should guarantee the effective exploitation of the prototyping efforts, ensuring that all the proposed representations can be identified and located and that the architectural solutions included in earlier prototyping projects can subsequently be exploited. Likewise, it is a good idea to report the wireframe history in the final project report, showing their evolution in relation to the discussions held.

Based on information gathered from benchmarking strategies, it is also advisable to adopt best practices and to avoid the bad architectural practices of existing websites that are similar to the one under development. This means that after analyzing competitors' webpages, common architectural elements, and those that users are used to seeing and using, should be incorporated into the prototypes. The incorporation of these common elements should facilitate the subsequent use of the Website and ultimately ensure that the site is more useful. However, the incorporation of these elements should be undertaken without forgetting that, as mentioned in the analysis phase, for the Website being developed there are many different types of user who will have different skills and levels of information literacy.

Finally, it is a good idea to ensure that the wireframes incorporate elements of interaction and that they respect accessibility standards (Wodtke, 2009). By incorporating a certain degree of interactivity (if, for example, they are navigable via the activation of the links they incorporate), they will facilitate communication and the discussion of the prototyping proposals with other professionals involved in developing the Website and it will also ensure that they can be used directly in tests with selected users when evaluating certain architectural elements (such as the navigation and organization systems, for example). Respecting accessibility standards in prototyping is a way of ensuring that the pages that will eventually be built using these prototypes also respect these standards and that the access of any kind of user is guaranteed, from the sensory point of view.

4.4 PROTOTYPING TOOLS

We turn now to look at the various techniques and tools that can be used to develop and implement Website diagramming or prototyping.

The simplest way of representing the prototype is to draw it using pencil and paper. With a pencil and paper, the general structure of the Website being developed can be represented together with each of the webpages and the content making up the site.

However, to facilitate the process, several products are available on the market. For example, we can find a series of templates in PDF format that can be used to create prototypes. An example of products of this kind can be found on the page of Konigi (http://konigi.com/tools/graph-paper). Similarly, other companies (including, for example, Web Design Sketchbook – webdesign-sketchbook.com) offer sketchbooks (and a downloadable version in PDF format) that provide ready printed versions of a browser framework to facilitate and simplify the drawing of prototypes, by incorporating this fixed element. Finally, other companies (including, for example, UI Stencils – uistencils.com) market plastic or metal templates that incorporate the main elements of the visual language for prototyping and that facilitate and standardize the drawing of each of these elements in proposals for blueprints and wireframes.

Yet, if our goal is to discuss various prototyping proposals in a team, then an interesting tool is one like that provided by Guimags (guimags.com). This company sells a series of magnets that can be stuck to the typical vinyl whiteboards used in meetings as designers work together to build prototypes. With these magnets, it is possible to represent most of the structural elements and controls (drop-down menus, buttons, scroll bars, etc.) that make up the webpages users eventually visualize. As various prototype proposals are discussed, the magnets can be reused and easily moved around, and their surface, like that of a vinyl whiteboard, can also be written on. The company also supplies square-grid vinyl boards to make using these magnets even easier.

However, besides these more basic tools for developing prototype proposals, there are a series of specific computerized tools that can greatly facilitate this task.

These prototyping tools or software applications usually include at least four features or functions: a library of objects, a representation of the site architecture (blueprint), an annotation system and a project management system.

The library of objects (or widgets) is used to represent the most common components of a webpage: navigation bars, search boxes, forms, blocks of text, etc. Normally objects can be dragged and dropped on to the canvas, where often their properties (colour, background, size, etc.) can be edited.

The representation of the site architecture (blueprint) shows the complete site map and the connections between the pages. Most of the programs generate this blueprint automatically as they create the site's new pages.

The annotation system allows the components of a page to be described, clarified and specified. Finally, the project management system includes a version history, user management system, and a tracking system linked to a calendar, among other utilities.

In addition, by combining or varying these four main functions, the tools can, for example, create dynamic wireframes, that is, with navigable links between the site's components or with external sites; freehand drawing systems; and formats that allow varying degrees of import and export, among other options.

Leaving aside tools exclusively designed for the prototyping of digital content for mobile devices (such as, Briefs, Flinto, Fluid and Form, among others), the leading computerized solutions for architectural Website design can be classified into two main types: desktop tools and online tools.

4.4.1 Desktop Tools

There is a wide range of desktop tools (commercial or free) on the market that are used by professionals dedicated to interaction design, in general, and information architecture, in particular, for the creation of Website prototyping.

However, among these, several desktop solutions stand out for the quality of their features and their popularity in the community of web designers: Axure, Visio, OmniGraffle, Justinmind, ConceptDraw Pro, Denim and Pencil Project. They constitute a set of solutions (some commercial, others free) that can be used both for prototyping webs and apps for mobile devices.

4.4.1.1 Axure

Axure (http://www.axure.com) (as well as Visio) is one of the most popular commercial tools among information designers and architects.

This is a desktop tool specifically designed for prototyping web environments (wireframes and blueprints). It has traditionally served as a graphical solution for computers using a Windows operating system although, given the size of the market, a version for computers run on the Apple operating system has been developed.

If we turn to look at its features, it is a highly versatile tool allowing, in addition to the design of wireframes and blueprints, the generation of flowcharts based on the gallery of resources it offers. Note, however, that the interface of this tool is only available in English.

It incorporates a standard library housing all the classic graphic elements used in the design of webpage prototypes. The objects can be dragged directly from the library to the working document where they can then be edited and customized. The library allows all the available elements to be managed and edited as well as new external graphic components to be incorporated. It also allows the prototyping of applications for interactive mobile environments.

As for interacting with other tools, Axure allows the exportation of its prototyping proposals to the following formats: HTML, Word, Cvs, some image formats (Bitmap, PNG, JPG and GIF), JavaScript (which can be viewed in IE, Firefox, Safari and Chrome) and RP (Axure's own format).

Among the tool's strengths are the possibility it affords of including annotations and legends explaining the prototypes developed. These complementary options greatly facilitate the tasks of communication that the information architect has to undertake with, for example, the customer or the eventual developers of the Website. Axure also includes the possibility of creating and editing joint prototyping projects involving various architects, and it includes a version control system.

The prototypes created with this tool have the possibility of being dynamic and of facilitating interaction and navigation between their content pages.

The official Website of the tool includes a large library of wireframe templates and blueprints, tutorials to learn how to get the most out of the tool, a blog where the latest news and the developments of new versions are discussed, a support space including FAQs about the product, and even a highly dynamic forum where the community of tool users can participate and clarify together all the doubts that might arise when implementing the tool.

4.4.1.2 Visio

The commercial tool Visio (https://products.office.com/visio/flowchart-software) was acquired by Microsoft in 2000. Prior to that date, although it included other capabilities, it was essentially a desktop application to support technical drawing in engineering and architecture projects. Since then, Microsoft's strategy for this tool has centred on the development and promotion of its other graphical display capabilities.

Without abandoning completely its engineering capabilities (such as circuits, fluids and control systems) and its architectural capabilities (such as site and floor plans), Microsoft has opted explicitly to develop graphical displays for firms (organizational charts, brainstorming diagrams, flowcharts, etc.), for project management (Gantt and PERT charts, for example) and for prototyping websites (such as blueprints and wireframes). This shift in direction has greatly increased the versatility of this solution compared to other prototyping tools.

The tool allows users to work with its interface in various languages. The interface provides a standard library with around 50 graphic elements that are typically used in the design of Website prototypes. These elements can be directly incorporated from the library to the working document where they can be edited. The library can be upgraded by adding new graphic elements designed by external developers.

As for interacting with other tools, Visio allows the exportation of its prototyping proposals to the following formats: PDF, HTML, SGV, Auto-CAD, TIFF, JPEG, GIF, PNG as well as its own Visio format. When importing files, it supports, among other formats, HTML, SGV, AutoCAD, TIFF, JPEG, GIF, PNG and its own Visio format.

The tool offers the possibility of including annotations and legends explaining the prototypes designed and undertaking and editing prototyping projects in teams. Moreover, the tool facilitates the creation of dynamic prototypes and navigation between their content pages.

Finally, it is worth noting that the tool's official Website displays a large library of graphic templates, tutorial support, training videos, a section to make comments, and even some discussion groups where users can solve their doubts about how to use the tool.

4.4.1.3 OmniGraffle

OmniGraffle (www.omnigroup.com/applications/OmniGraffle) is one of the most popular commercial prototyping tools among information architects working in Apple's operating environment (OS and iOS). No versions are available for working with any other operating systems.

It is a highly versatile desktop tool designed for creating graphical representations in general, but it also allows the creation of prototyping for web environments (wireframes and blueprints). Note, however, that the interface of this tool is only available in English.

It does not incorporate a standard library of the classic graphic elements used in Website prototyping design. However, this is no problem as the library allows the user to manage and edit the elements available and to incorporate new external graphic components. So, it is not difficult to find and incorporate the necessary elements for web prototyping, for example, from its own official page or from pages of third–party developers (http://konigi.com/tools/omnigraffle-wireframe-stencils and http://uxkits.com/products/website-flowchart-and-sitemap, for example). As with the other tools analyzed, these graphic elements are easy to use, as they can be dragged directly from the library to the working document and then edited as desired.

In the same way as Visio, OmniGraffle offers a wide range of possibilities for interacting with other tools. This graphics solution allows prototyping proposals to be exported to different formats including, for example, Omni-Graffle, PDF, TIFF, PNG, JPEG, EPS, HTML, OmniOutliner, SVG, PICT, Photoshop, BMP and Visio. It also allows the direct importation of files in different formats including, among others, OmniGraffle, Visio, DOT, Diagram 2, Xcode and EOModeler.

In common with the two previous tools, OmniGraffle offers the possibility of including annotations and legends explaining the prototypes developed and also the possibility of creating and editing prototyping projects in teams.

The prototypes created with this tool can be dynamic and allow interaction and navigation between their content pages. On the official Website of this graphics solution there is a large library of graphic templates, video tutorials offering help in using the tool, a space for user support, and also a forum to solve collaboratively the possible doubts and performance problems that the user might encounter.

4.4.1.4 Justinmind

Justinmind (justinmind.com) is another highly popular commercial proto-typing tool among information architects. It is available both for Windows and Apple operating systems.

It is a highly flexible desktop tool designed for creating web prototyping environments (wireframes and blueprints, including responsive designs), apps (Android and iOS), enterprise apps, and, even cards for Google Glass apps.

It has a similar aesthetic to other solutions, including Photoshop and Illustrator, and it offers, in addition to these diagramming types, various capabilities related to interaction. It facilitates interaction with prototypes for webs and mobile apps (Android and iOS), mobile gestures and transitions. Visually, it permits image synchronization with Photoshop, integration (copy/paste as SVG file) with Adobe Illustration, and it allows images to be dragged and dropped directly from the browser or file system. In the case of simulation, it enables integration with user testing tools and services, and emulates Android and iOS (iPhone and iPad) mobile environments for testing.

Like the tools already discussed, Justinmind allows the export of proto-typing proposals to different formats including, for example, HTML + JS and PDF, generating documentation in MS Word and Open Office formats. Interestingly, it can also automatically generate the site map from the wireframes developed.

It also offers the possibility of including annotations and legends in the prototypes developed and also the possibility of creating and editing proto-typing projects in a team.

4.4.1.5 ConceptDraw Pro

ConceptDraw Pro (www.conceptdraw.com) is a highly versatile commercial desktop application oriented, primarily, at diagramming and graphical display for business environments (including, organizational charts, brainstorming diagrams, flowcharts and project management) but it also includes graphic capabilities for prototyping websites (both blueprints and wireframes) and mobile apps. This graphic display solution is available in versions for Windows platforms and the Apple operating system.

The solution offers a standard library of the most frequently used graphic elements in the prototyping of websites and apps. As with the previous tools, these items can be moved directly from the library to the working document, where they can be edited as desired. The library can be upgraded with new external graphic elements that can be found, for example, on its own official page. Interestingly, this tool incorporates a Site Mapper Wizard option, which, by indicating the corresponding URL, automatically generates the blueprint or site map of an existing web.

As for its interaction with other tools, ConceptDraw Pro allows its prototyping proposals to be exported to different formats, including PDF, HTML, XML, PowerPoint, Macromedia Flash, the main graphic formats, SVG and its own ConceptDraw format. As for importing files, it supports among other formats, XML, the main graphic formats, PowerPoint, BMP, Visio and its own ConceptDraw format.

The solution includes the option of dropping annotations and facilitates the inclusion of explanatory legends for the prototypes designed. It also enables the designing and editing of prototyping projects in teams. It is worth stressing too that this tool supports the creation of dynamic prototypes and permits navigation between their content pages.

Finally, it should be noted that the tool's official Website includes a large library of graphic templates, tutorial help and a support space.

4.4.1.6 Denim

Denim (dub.washington.edu:2007/projects/denim) is a simple desktop tool specifically developed for prototyping user interfaces. It emerged as a project from the Human – Computer Interaction and Design Group at the University of Washington.

Denim is a free solution available for computers operating on Windows, Unix and Mac OS X platforms. It can be downloaded directly from its official Website, where the source code can also be found. The tool only offers the possibility of working with an English interface.

Although it is a highly intuitive tool and the user will find they hardly have to consult the support documents to begin putting it to use, the solution is very poor in terms of the features it offers. In addition to prototyping, users can develop flowcharts and storyboards. However, its library of graphic elements for the prototyping of webpages is very limited. These widgets can be used by moving them directly from the library to the working document, but any postediting is again very limited. Unfortunately, the library cannot be upgraded with any new external graphics.

As for interacting with other tools, it only allows prototyping proposals in HTML or in its own Denim format to be exported. In the case of importing files, it only supports those in its own format.

While the tool allows the user to create dynamic, navigable prototypes, the solution does not offer the possibility of directly dropping annotations and legends to explain aspects of the prototypes nor does it allow teams to work collaboratively on prototype designs.

It is worth pointing out that while no wireframes or blueprints appear on the tool's official Website, support documentation with practical exercises can be found, together with a section for further support and comments, and even a mailing list where questions can be put to other users to see if they can help solve problems that arise.

4.4.1.7 Pencil Project

Pencil Project (pencil.evolus.vn) is the last desktop tool for Website prototyping that we will review here. It is a free, open-source GUI solution available for all platforms, including Apple, Windows and GNU/Linux. It can also be installed as an add-on into the Firefox browser. The tool only offers the possibility of using an English interface.

It is a highly versatile solution that, among other graphic representations, enables the development of wireframes, blueprints and apps for Android and iOS. For this it provides a library holding more than 50 graphic elements for designing Website prototypes. These elements are used as with the other tools, importing them directly from the library to the working document where they can later be edited. The library can also be upgraded with new external graphics.

As for its interactivity with other tools, it allows users to export their prototyping proposals to different formats including, for example, HTML, Png, OpenOffice, Word, PDF and its Pencil format. However, it only allows the direct import of files already in the Pencil format.

The solution enables the creation of dynamic and navigable prototypes and the inclusion of annotations. However, it does not offer the possibility of including legends or of developing and editing prototyping projects in teams.

The official Website of the tool offers similar resources to those available on the sites of the other desktop tools analyzed here. For instance, the user can find examples and templates of wireframes, blueprints and mobile apps, support tutorials and even a wiki space.

4.4.2 Online Tools

In recent years a wide range of applications have appeared based on so-called cloud computing, that is, applications launched from a browser without the need to install additional software.

For some companies and professionals this represents an important advantage because it avoids having to install and maintain programs on the firm's computers. In addition, the data and documents created with these applications are automatically stored on Internet servers, so they can be accessed from any computer on the planet. For this same reason, they all enable designers to collaborate and work in teams, in some cases with the additional resources of synchronous communication systems, such as chat, and even of online user testing systems. Naturally, these are all functions that desktop applications, by definition, cannot compete with.

Additionally, when launched on any standard browser (such as Chrome, Explorer, Safari or Mozilla), these applications are in effect operating independently of the user's platform (Windows, Linux, Apple, etc.).

It should come as no surprise therefore to learn that there are many online applications for Website prototyping. However, in general, these online tools are less sophisticated than desktop applications. Yet, at the same time, online programs are generally cheaper (available via subscription) and some versions (typically providing basic access) are even available at zero cost.

A broad range of online tools are available for use by professionals of interaction design, in general, and information architecture, in particular. The online solutions include, among others, such tools as Pidoco, Lovely Chart, Mocking-Bird, iPlotz and Lumzy. However, thanks to their functionality and features, the following four stand out: MockFlow, invision, Marvel and proto.io.

4.4.2.1 MockFlow

MockFlow (www.mockflow) is a commercial online application for the design of user interfaces, including software products in general, but the tool provides specialized features for prototyping websites. Indeed, it is one of the most comprehensive products thanks to these specialized features.

It offers a particularly elegant interface, it is highly intuitive to use and enables the rapid creation of prototypes. It is also one of the applications that provides the greatest number of widgets, both standard and for mobiles.

It offers almost everything one would expect from a specialized prototyping program: version control, real-time collaboration, annotations, scheme-based design, importation of predefined schemes, generation of web maps, use of grids, among many other features. Finally, it is worth noting that it is one of the tools that offers a free version (basic access) without any functional restrictions, except for the number of projects and the number of pages in each project.

4.4.2.2 InVision

InVision (invisionapp.com) is another powerful commercial online application specialized in prototyping. It enables the design of interactive diagramming for both web environments and mobile applications.

Among its many strengths, it is worth stressing the ease with which it can be learned and its user friendliness, the possibilities it provides for intuitive file (drag-and-drop) management, its presentation system and the ability it affords to communicate and collaborate in real time, its automatic version control features and project synchronization, the option of adding animations in page transitions in mobile prototypes as well as support for mobile gestures in prototypes of this kind.

It also offers a free, full-featured, version for use on a single project, and a plan for use in educational environments.

4.4.2.3 Marvel

Marvel (marvelapp.com), like the previous solutions, is a commercial tool that enables the online design of interactive diagramming for web environments and mobile applications.

It is a simple, intuitive tool that users quickly become familiar with. Among its best features is the possibility of creating prototypes from previously created mocks, importing them from Dropbox and then keeping them in sync. It also facilitates working in collaboration with colleagues, making comments and dropping annotations, and it supports basic gestures in prototypes for mobile environments and simple animations in page transitions. It also includes the option to embed prototypes into a Website and to export diagrams made in formats that include PDF, ZIP, APK (Android) or IPA (iOS).

It should be stressed though that the interactivity and animations are quite limited, and that some of its functions (such as adding hotspots to multiple screens) are hard to discover. Like the other tools, a free version is available with a number of functional limitations such as the number of users and the prototype export format.

4.4.2.4 Proto.io

The final commercial online tool for prototyping that we will review in this chapter is proto.io (proto.io). Among its capabilities we stress the tool's good training resources and support documentation, file synchronization via Dropbox, prototyping for Apple Watch and a library of material design elements. It also allows the user to add touch events, mouse events, device orientation, animation features and screen transitions to their prototyping.

Projects can be exported and archived in PDF, PNGs and HTML. It allows users to copy and paste between projects and supports the team creation of prototypes, with feedback comments and a version control system. A free, full-featured version of this tool can be used for 15 days, and monthly payment plans are available depending on the number of users and active projects under development.

PART TWO

Findability and Search Experience Optimization

CHAPTER 5

The Essentials of Search Engine Optimization

5.1 INTRODUCTION

In earlier chapters we have had the opportunity to examine various architectural features of a Website's navigation system that enable the user to access its content efficiently, even sites with a large volume of content. In this chapter we look at the essentials of Website positioning, or search engine optimization (SEO), that is, the guidelines and best practices that ensure a Website is visible on the World Wide Web. First, we present a brief description of SEO; then we focus on one of its principal objects of study, namely search engines; and finally we analyze Website positioning factors.

5.2 WHAT IS SEARCH ENGINE OPTIMIZATION?

SEO comprises that set of professional activities and objects of study whose purpose is to understand, first, how Internet search engines work and, second, how to make a Website as visible as possible.

These two goals are closely related because to achieve the latter, that is, boosting a webpage's visibility, we need to know how search engines calculate the relevance of information when they order the results of user searches.

The rationale for the above is based on the way in which internauts tend to behave. For most people, seeking information on the web means using a search engine like Google, Bing or DuckDuckGo. And this coincides with the fact that a very high proportion of Website traffic is generated by the results of search engines.

Finally, there is a third element, which is closely tied to the above, that is, that most users do not look beyond the first page of search engine results. This means that if a Website does not appear on this first page of the search engine results for certain keywords, it loses visibility and with it a part of its traffic.

For content-intensive sites, the loss of a share of this traffic, even if it is only a few percentage points, is a serious problem, because they need this traffic to capture more advertising, increase their market share or achieve greater prestige, among other goals.

Navigation Design and SEO for Content-Intensive Websites
ISBN 978-0-08-100676-4

Obvious examples of this are news media sites that need the greatest possible visibility to attract advertisers and subscribers; university Websites that need to make their degree courses, master's and PhD programmes known to their potential students; and the leading museums in each country that need to boost their web positioning to justify their policies of cultural diffusion. Finally, e-commerce Websites clearly need to optimize the pages of their catalogues to reach the sales figures that make their businesses viable. However, as the reader will be aware by now, here we focus on content-intensive sites, as typified by the first three cases mentioned herein.

This explains why when the pages of a Website tend to appear on the first page of the search results (at least for certain keywords), we say that the site is well positioned. Or, another way of saying the same thing, and it is critical to bear this in mind, is to say that the site is search engine optimized. This is important, as we shall see later on, because in content-intensive sites, especially news media sites, a contradiction sometimes occurs between being optimized for search engines (or for robots, so to speak) and being optimized for human users. Next, we look at how search engines work before considering the principal factors of positioning.

5.3 HOW SEARCH ENGINES WORK

Search engines are the most important document information systems of our time. They form a fundamental part of the Internet landscape, although in recent years social networks like Facebook and Twitter have eroded some of their importance. Whatever the case, no one today could imagine exploiting the immense wealth of the Web without the help of a search engine, the functions of which have not ceased to grow or undergo changes since their appearance in the 1990s.

One way of understanding the functions of a search engine is to see it as a kind of information system, which can be represented diagrammatically, as shown in Fig. 5.1.

In line with this diagram, we can see that an information system (such as a search engine) accepts two kinds of input: documents and information needs. The documents in this case are primarily webpages, and the information needs are expressed via the questions posed by the internauts. The system output is a list of Websites that, presumably, contain information that can satisfy the information needs of the user and, hence, the output is labelled with the (perhaps optimistic) title of 'People informed'.

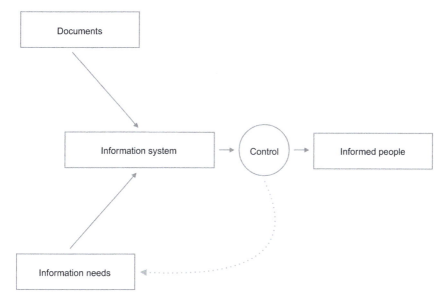

Figure 5.1 Diagram of a document information system.

Naturally, if the first query does not provide satisfactory results, the user (or the internaut) will logically make another attempt. This is represented by the ellipse labelled with the word 'Control'. In other words, it is assumed that the user examines the relevance of the results and if he is not satisfied, he repeats the question using other terms or introducing some other kind of change.

5.3.1 Structure

A search engine comprises a coordinated set of programs that work together. These programs can be classified in two main groups: the system of exploration or the web crawlers (or web spiders) and the information retrieval system. However, each of these systems is made up of a number of subsystems (Fig. 5.2).

5.3.1.1 *Web Crawler*

The web crawler, or system of exploration, has the mission of discovering and downloading webpages and other Internet documents. To do so, it uses a list of URLs or webpage addresses (1). From these it can access documents (2) published on the Web and download these documents (mostly webpages, but also office documents, presentations or image files, among others) in the data warehouse or document repository of the search engine (3). The web crawler obtains new URLs (4) from the downloaded pages, which it adds to its list of URLs awaiting analysis (5).

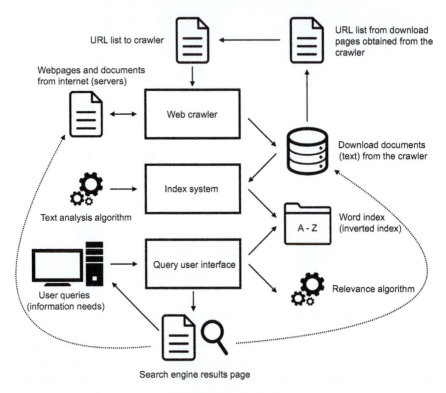

Figure 5.2   Structure and functions of a search engine.

5.3.1.2 Information Retrieval System

The information retrieval system is also made up of two components: the indexing system and the query system. The first of these is in charge of analyzing the documents downloaded from the Web and with the creating of indexes that then allow search queries to be made; while the second is the search engine's visible interface, that is, the part with which users interact.

If a search engine is able to answer questions in such astonishingly short spaces of time as we have become accustomed to (typically, fractions of a second), it is because they do not explore the Web for users in real time (that is, as and when the query is made), but rather they use an index that is updated regularly (several times a day).

A system that attempted to explore the documents on the Web sequentially and in real-time to provide answers would not make the slightest bit of sense. Days or even weeks could pass between the question being asked and an answer being given. Instead of this, what a search engine does is to query its internal indexes.

Document Nº	Content
00001	Title: Proactive Marketing for the New and Experienced Library Director Authors: Melissa Goldsmith & Anthony Fonseca
00002	Title: Digital Information Strategies: From Applications and Content to Libraries and People
...	...
34567	Title: Research 2.0 and the Future of Information Literacy

Figure 5.3 A direct index.

5.3.1.3 Direct Indexes

Search engines use at least two types of indexes, known as direct and inverted indexes. Queries are resolved by inverted indexes, while direct indexes, which are the ones we shall look at first, are used as internal elements of management and control.

A direct index provides us with a list of documents (or records) in chronological order (with the oldest document first, for example) or numerical order (from document number one through to the last). Fig. 5.3 illustrates this type of index.

As we can see, with this index, to determine whether a document exists with the terms 'research' and 'information literacy', we would have to browse through tens of thousands of index entries (specifically, 34567 in the example in our simulation). It would be even worse, though, if the full index contained, for example, a hundred thousand entries, then we would have to browse through all the entries to determine whether there was more than one document that fulfilled the above condition.

As can easily be imagined, indexes of this kind are not much of an improvement on the real-time Web crawling with which we speculated earlier. As such, a search engine needs to complement this index with an inverted index, which is in fact what is used to respond to queries (while the direct index is used for internal management and administration).

5.3.1.4 Inverted Indexes

The structure of an inverted index is the exact inverse of the direct index (hence its name); that is, it stores an ordered list of each of the words that occur in the different documents and associated with the specific documents in which they occur. The typical structure of an inverted index, therefore, can be depicted as in Fig. 5.4.

The index operates as follows:

- In the column headed 'Single term' appear the different words that occur in the documents, but there is only one row for each word (although in the set of documents this word may occur many times).
- The 'Frequency' column records the total number of times each term occurs.
- Finally, under 'Location' appears a key in the form of a vector indicating the document number, the zone or field in which the word occurs and the word order. There is a vector for each occurrence.

If we take the term 'Research', we can see how this works in more detail. In this case, the 'Frequency' column gives a reading of '110', which means that the term 'Research' occurs 110 times in the set of documents, and that we will therefore have 110 different vectors in the 'Location' column. The table shows just one of these for the sake of simplicity.

If we now take this vector [(34567, 01, 01)], the first number, 34567, identifies the document, and the second, 01, identifies the zone or field of the document in which the word occurs, in this case, the 'Title'.

Single term	Frequency	Location
Research	110	(34567, 01, 01),...
...	...	...
Goldsmith	233	(00001, 02, 01),...
...	...	...
...	...	...
Information literacy	214	(34567, 01, 03),...
...	...	...

Figure 5.4 An inverted index.

Other auxiliary indexes help the search engine to browse the list of single terms using a small number of comparison operations. The best thing is that indexes of this kind ensure the response time is virtually independent of the number of terms that appear on the list.

The main shortcoming of these indexes, however, is the amount of hardware they require, particularly, if they have to serve millions of users simultaneously, as is the case of search engines.

It is readily deduced that Google can assign a maximum amount of memory to each user, and, so, it cannot load all the information from its indexes. A technical solution here is never to load more than n references in memory for each query, and hence this limitation.

In order for the search engine to build an index, it needs a procedure that allows it to analyze the webpages and to extract the terms from them that will make up the index, and to do this it needs to determine what is and what is not a term.

The simplest algorithm would determine that a term is a string of characters between blank spaces. However, this algorithm would produce many errors. For example, it would not select the words at the beginning of each sentence or know how to deal with those surrounded by punctuation marks; nor would it be useful for identifying words without meaning, such as pronouns or articles, to name but a few.

5.3.1.5 Query Interface

The query interface carries out the following functions: first, the query form sends the question to another part of the system in order to compare the terms of the question with the inverted index and, thus, to filter the webpages containing the terms of the question.

Second, the search engine has to present the results as clearly and efficiently as possible on the so-called search engine results page (SERP).

Finally, but perhaps most importantly, the results have to be displayed in some meaningful order, which means we can immediately rule out chronological or alphabetical order, given their limited value in such a heterogeneous context and the vast amount of documents on the Internet. It is here that the so-called relevance calculation algorithm comes into its own. The rest of this section looks at this algorithm in more detail.

5.3.1.6 Relevance Calculation

In the information retrieval process, all documents are considered as having a different degree of relevance for each question or information need. For any given question, at one extreme we have the documents with zero relevance (as they are totally unrelated to the question), while at the other extreme we (hopefully) have documents whose relevance is total (or almost total). Between the two extremes we have documents with varying degrees of relevance.

If we express this relevance in percentage terms, we have a spectrum that runs from 0% to 100%, with documents in between that are, for example, 10%, 25% or 70% relevant.

The most logical procedure would be to present the results page with the documents ranked according to their degree of relevance. In this way, even though there might be thousands and thousands of relevant documents in the response, we are able to limit ourselves to consulting the first 10 or 20, given that we can assume these to be the most relevant. Other systems, such as alphabetical or chronological order, would not be as economical in terms of time, since to ensure that we were accessing the most relevant documents we would have to examine the whole list.

Existing search engines often combine two sets of criteria to determine a Website's relevance: internal criteria (OnPage) and external criteria (OffPage).

OnPage Criteria

Internal criteria refer primarily to the content and, therefore, to statistical aspects such as the frequency of occurrence of the keyword (or words) in the question. Specifically, webpages with the highest keyword density will be the most relevant, provided that this frequency is not unnatural, that is, that it is not due to an overoptimization of the search engine function, since this is something existing browsers detect. When the terms on a page occur at a higher frequency than they do in natural language, search engines detect that the page is fraudulent or of poor quality.

For this reason, the statistical frequency should be related to occurrences in content of quality. Therefore, the internal aspects refer quite simply to the quality of the site's content, that is, the content of both its texts and multimedia components.

Other aspects, such as the fact that the keyword appears surrounded by <h1> or <h2> tags, that is, to form part of the page's title or subtitles, also gives greater relevance to the corresponding page, as does the fact that the keyword forms part of the page's URL.

Other critical aspects include the quality of the source code (use of standards), the use of metadata such as those corresponding to the <title> and <meta description> tags, and last but not least, designs that are compatible with the mobile web (responsive design).

OffPage Criteria

External criteria refer to the results that can be generated by analyzing the inbound links of the page being considered.

In theory, each search engine has its own sets of criteria and its own rules for assigning weights to each criterion, but in general, the characteristics of the links a page receives are usually one of the most important, at least as important as the other factors. Among these characteristics we should include the number of inbound links from quality Websites, the text used in the inbound link and the thematic relationship of the inbound links with the web topic (or topics), among others.

A readily established criterion is that a Website can be said to improve its position in relation to a search engine if it receives many inbound links from sites that, in turn, are highly linked and thematically related to the topic of the site under consideration.

In recent years, the increasing importance of social platforms has meant that so-called user signals are important, including the number of tweets a page receives, the number of mentions on the social web or 'likes' on Facebook, among others.

5.3.1.7 Results Page

Finally, the search engine's response in the shape of a ranked list of documents has to be presented. The search engine results page or SERP is responsible for this.

The functions of the SERP, other than the fact that we can click on the results shown there, usually go unnoticed, given that at first glance it only provides a list of pages or documents. However, a careful look at Google SERPs reveals the following information and options:
- Total number of pages containing the keyword;
- The paid or sponsored listings;
- The unpaid listings (or organic search results). In this case, for each of these results, we have a snippet or summary with the following information:
  - title of the page (or document)
  - document type (when it is not HTML)
  - two lines describing the document content
  - the page's URL

  As well as the following options:
- Obtain a translated version of the page using an automatic translation (that is, generally a very poor version);
- Search for pages with similar content;

- A sequential navigation among the results or a visit to a specific page of results (roughly as far as page 90 or so, or a maximum theoretical total of 900 results).

However, the position that a site obtains in the SERP also depends on user profiles, provided that Google is able to identify them (a previously identified user or via the cookies, etc.). In this case, the SERP not only uses the webpage characteristics but also a combination of these and the user characteristics (including previous search history, the user's profile on the web and their geographic location, etc.).

The point is that, in terms of usability, some believe Google SERP to be an excellent example of usability, thanks to the large amount of content that it is able to store without this ever representing a cognitive burden for the user to browse through.

From the perspective of SEO, obtaining a high ranking in the SERP is becoming more and more difficult given the competition to occupy these positions, especially as increasingly they have to be shared with other types of results from a range of different indexes: news, videos, maps etc. For this reason, studying and gaining a good understanding of the results pages of search engines is becoming an increasingly important task in the job profile of the SEO professional.

5.4 POSITIONING FACTORS

Earlier we have briefly seen the elements that a search engine considers when ranking the results. This allows us to understand how search engines do their job. Now we shall consider these same factors, but from the perspective of search engine optimization. That is, we shall consider them in more detail and we shall examine them from the point of view of the actions and checks that an SEO professional needs to bear in mind to optimize Website visibility.

5.4.1 Barriers

First, note that there are certain technical barriers that prevent a search engine from 'understanding' a site. The first of these that we need to be aware of is that search engines understand neither graphics, videos nor multimedia animations made with Flash or any other alternative technology. In general, they do not understand anything that is not text, which is not to say that a Website should only have text, since it would not work very well – on the contrary, multimedia applications are essential.

As should have been gathered from the previous discussion, the main barrier to the SEO of a site is the site itself – if it has no content of interest, how can it expect to attract traffic? No one would claim that this is easy to achieve. On the contrary, it accounts for the main part of a site's maintenance budget, now that the technological concerns of maintenance have become much easier to address thanks to the development of content management systems.

Other barriers may be attributable to the technology used to encode the site and that prevents the search engines from interpreting it. For example, the site might use a lot of graphics and little text, or use obsolete techniques like Frames, or incorrectly use technologies such as JavaScript or Flash, which prevent the search engines from exploring a site properly as it lacks textual content.

5.4.2 The Basic Checklist

Following, we present a checklist of the essential aspects required to optimize Website positioning. As we noted, it is usual to distinguish between OnPage and OffPage positioning factors, that is, those that are under our control and those that we cannot control (or at least, not entirely).

In a previous section we summarized these factors from the point of view of the tasks of a search engine. Now we do so in more detail and from the perspective of the interests of a professional or a student of SEO. In the following list we identify them together with a description.

5.4.2.1 OnPage Factors
Site Theme and Content
The Website content must clearly focus on the site's main theme via the use of textual content, but without neglecting additional multimedia elements.

Some time ago now it was estimated that a site should have between 30 and 50 pages of good textual content related to the site's main theme (Ramos & Cota, 2006). Today this number must have easily doubled and a site should have at least 60 to 100 pages. Other recent estimations (for example, from the plugin manufacturer Yoast SEO) recommend that each page should include at least 300 words to ensure its importance. Naturally, there are differences between each sector, and growing competition means that highly competitive sectors increasingly need a greater volume of content.

Original, Quality Content
From the previous information it can be deduced that a site cannot expect to be well positioned if the search engines do not have anything with which

to position it. In other words, it needs content. But in today's web any old content will simply not do. It must meet various conditions: it must be original, high in quality, plentiful and up to date.

The content needs to be original, but not in the sense of quirky or unusual, rather it should not have been taken from somewhere else and it should not be duplicated in other sections or elsewhere on other pages of the Website. Some of the latest Google algorithms are dedicated precisely to preventing pages from appearing at the top of the rankings if they detect a lot of duplicate content, ie, repeated or copied from other sites.

The content needs to be high in quality; there is no place for mediocre content. The web is full of good quality content, well-designed and presented, rich in information and data from carefully conducted studies or highly selective content curation practices. For a site to stand out in a highly competitive environment, it has to publish content of the highest quality.

The content should also be plentiful and updated on a regular basis, that is, new content should be frequently incorporated. Additionally, the content should be well edited, enriched with multimedia elements and not overly mixed with intrusive advertising. Specifically, another of Google's latest algorithms is specialized in detecting pages with poor content, as well as pages that are overoptimized for SEO or that contain excessive advertising.

Multimedia Content

It is very difficult to be well positioned without any multimedia content, that is, without any photographs, graphics, videos or infographics.

A site needs a content-creating policy for the topics it deals with that incorporates multimedia materials: videos (tutorials, for example, or product demonstrations), images (photographs of products and installations) and infographics (advice, sector studies and technical skills, etc.).

Modern, Attractive Design

Successful Websites follow very strict design guidelines. There are clear trends in current design that favour large images, very clear typography, an abundance of white, a variety of typefaces and varied colours, but well combined, attractive navigation systems with a good balance between the various elements.

Fortunately, if we work with a content management system (CMS), such as WordPress, we can find themes with excellent designs at affordable prices. That is, today, a Website can look good and be well designed on a budget accessible to a small or medium-sized organization; even nonprofit organizations can now afford to support their causes.

Information Architecture and Labelling

As we have seen in previous chapters, site architecture should be designed using user-centred systems, such as personas, scenarios and card sorting.

The navigation categories should be clear and understandable, and site navigation should be intuitive and highly consistent. A good system of categories and labels serves as a foundation for an associated navigation system that retains users and reduces bounce rates.

CMSs, such as WordPress, make it very easy to manage and add tags (keywords) and categories (classes) to a site's pages. The use of these tags and categories means pages of the same theme can be associated with each page, and so navigation using links to related posts can be improved. As we have stressed, this helps retain visitors and improves positioning.

Keywords

The keywords that express the business or themes of the site should be well represented in the site's content pages and strategically distributed in its titles (h1, h2 tags, etc.) and bold text links, but as naturally as possible, that is, without repeating these keywords in a meaningless way, which would be considered a case of overoptimization of the SEO and penalized by Google. They should also be in the site's taxonomy – navigation categories and labels, as well as in the internal URL.

URL

Ideally, the site URL should contain some of the site's essential keywords. For example, an art history site should have a URL like the following: www.arthistory.com. The site's navigation structure, the names of the menu items, and the URLs of individual pages should also bear the SEO in mind and use URLs with content keywords. URLs automatically generated by strings of meaningless characters should be avoided; what is needed are quite short URLs with keywords forming part of them.

Metadata and Source Code

Although they do not have a huge impact on positioning, the <title> and <meta description> metadata are essential because they form part of the SERP snippet. Therefore, their importance is great in terms of the SERP click-through rate. The better the snippet, the more clicks the site will get on the SERP. And there is considerable consensus that Google tends to penalize pages that obtain a low SERP click-through rate.

As for the source code, as we will no doubt be working with a CMS like WordPress or similar, what we need to do is ensure that our CMS uses HTML5 and a responsive design for compatibility with the mobile web.

Adaptation to the Mobile Web

For some time now sites have been receiving a major share of their traffic from the mobile web (especially from smartphones). Some kinds of sites, such as hotels and restaurants, as well as many local businesses, receive more traffic from mobile devices than from desktops.

In content-intensive sites, such as those of the news media, this trend is also being seen, and it is only a matter of time before it reaches museums and universities. Moreover, Google claims that it penalizes sites that are not adapted to the mobile web through the use of a responsive system. This point links up closely with the previous section examining the source code.

Maintaining the URL

Changing the URL gives bad results. The sites that maintain the same URL over the years benefit from this by obtaining a better positioning. If there is no alternative but to change the URL, then a careful policy has to be adopted with regard to redirections from the old URL to the new to minimize the impact.

Frame- or Flash-Based Navigation

It is essential at all costs to avoid using Frames or Flash technology to implement a site's navigation options. Use cascading style sheets (CSSs).

It should not be forgotten that search engines do not understand graphics and that a great animation in Flash only serves its purpose if it does not directly replace text and of course it helps the search engines and users understand the site. In any case, increasingly, Flash is discouraged and HTML5-based solutions are recommended instead.

5.4.2.2 OffPage Factors

Inbound Links

Despite the loss of importance suffered by PageRank, it is very important to obtain the maximum number of links from other sites. If the site provides relevant content and renews it frequently, other links are sure to arrive, but greater investment is increasingly required here to ensure success.

Depth of Indexing

Search engines need to integrate the maximum number of pages of a site in their index. Checks should be made with the search engines and the server's analytical tools to correct potential problems with the search engines' site indexing.

Network Presence and User Signals

Social networks and user signals emanating from them are essential input for search engine positioning algorithms. The inbound links from social networks are becoming increasingly influential both in traffic and positioning.

Publishing high-quality content that is not promoted via the social networks is to do things by halves. Until the content is 'moving' in the networks and it is being cited, and tweets are being sent, or it is being commented on and receiving 'likes', etc., it is as if it had a clandestine existence. Ideally, a CMS should be used to facilitate the dissemination of content via dynamic (independent) pages with inbuilt buttons that encourage the content to be shared in the networks easily (and automatically), along with the community management actions that can be carried out.

Traffic

The volume of Website traffic attracted also affects the positioning, in what is something of a vicious circle. Promotional activities within and outside the webpage therefore always make sense.

5.5 CONCLUSIONS

The opportunities available to a company that runs a Website for its target audience with a lot of interesting content are numerous. Moreover, content-intensive sites, such as those of the news media, museums and universities, are in a particularly advantageous position as their sites naturally produce quality, socially valuable information as part of their activities. And it is precisely this content that ensures a good SEO for a site.

The problem is that the objectives of positioning inevitably include changes in the coding of the page and the search for opportunities to obtain inbound links but, before all this, they even include changes in the strategic orientation of the content, and any tangible results in this regard will not be noticed until at least several weeks and, more likely, several months have passed.

At the very least this will mean an investment in time (people in the organization producing content as part of their work) and, in all probability, an investment in both time and money (content production outsourced to third parties, or recruitment of staff, albeit part time, to produce content).

Having an understanding of the structural and functional aspects that we have presented in this chapter will undoubtedly help SEO professionals and students improve these opportunities. Knowing a little better the basics of search engines will help in carrying out better searches, but undoubtedly, it will also help in developing Websites that are better adapted to search engines, and of course, it should help in developing better positioning campaigns.

CHAPTER 6

SEO for Content-Intensive Sites

6.1 INTRODUCTION

Having reviewed the essentials of search engine optimization (SEO), in this chapter we are ready to consider the different phases that make up a positioning campaign. After that, we focus our attention on aspects of OnSite SEO and, in particular, on content-based SEO, as this is one of the strengths of CISs.

Specifically, we present the main phases of a SEO campaign. But once these phases of the campaign have been implemented, the only way to sustain the site's position is by promoting a continuous policy of content creation and publishing.

To meet our objectives here, we also present a framework proposal to optimize site content linked to the production of news and current affairs, given that this is one of the most characteristic cases of CISs. However, this proposal can be extended to all the other CISs that we have referred to throughout this book (that is, not only news media sites but also university and museum Websites).

6.2 PHASES OF AN SEO CAMPAIGN

The SEO process has become increasingly more and more dynamic. It comprises a number of different phases that are conventionally referred to as its 'life cycle' but, in fact, Website positioning is never terminated. This is because changes in the Website itself and in the search engine algorithms, together with the emergence of new competitors, mean a site's positioning has to be constantly monitored and this, in turn, should foster new optimization activities.

The life cycle is, on occasions, referred to as a 'campaign', particularly when we wish to stress the need to reset the positioning cycle. For the sake of conceptual clarity, in this chapter, we present a complete overview of this cycle for a site that is considering aspects of SEO for the first time. We believe that this perspective readily admits the variations encountered both in sites created ex novo and in preexisting sites, that is, those that perhaps

Navigation Design and SEO for Content-Intensive Websites
ISBN 978-0-08-100676-4
125

have previously implemented positioning campaigns but which, for some reason, want to review or reconsider their SEO strategies.

The phases of the campaign can be described as adhering to the formula '3 + 1', because it includes three development phases plus one monitoring phase that may, eventually, lead us back to square one. To present these stages we follow the general principle of development based on the three universal phases of all projects, namely: analysis, design and implementation. Thus, we focus on the following phases: site analysis and an analysis of our main competitor, OnSite and OffSite strategy design, and implementation of the proposals adopted.

Sometime after the implementation of these phases (at least a month), a fourth phase needs to be implemented: an analysis of the site's positioning and a new comparative analysis of our competitors.

Up to this point, we have been talking about the site as a whole, and indeed it is a good idea to consider it in this way. Yet, as we know a site consists of pages and other kinds of documents (for example, reports in PDF format). For the purposes of positioning, the main unit of analysis is the pages, and it is the sum of the positioning of the individual pages of the site that gives us most of the overall SEO for a site. Certainly, a number of global factors, such as the age of the domain and the URL of the primary domain, are also relevant, but we insist that the SEO of a Website is the sum of the SEO of its individual pages.

Therefore, no site, least of all a CIS, can limit its optimization to that of the homepage. There is another reason for this, namely, given the nature of the Web, there is absolutely no reason why we should assume that visitors to a site access it via its homepage. Following these clarifications, we can now focus on each phase of the positioning life cycle or campaign.

6.2.1 Analysis Phase

In this phase we perform a double analysis: first, we examine the words that can do most to boost our site content; and second, we examine the sites of our competition.

6.2.1.1 Keyword Analysis

Recall that the query terms employed by search engine users are known as keywords. By the same measure, the terms that occur in a site's content, and which may eventually match the words employed by users when they perform their searches, are also known as keywords. Of course, keywords are also the terms that appear in search engine indexes.

A keyword can be a simple word (eg 'Art') or a compound expression (eg, 'Art History'). It might be a common noun ('museum') or a proper noun ('Louvre'). It might express a concept ('beauty') or something tangible ('houses'). It might also correspond to branches of knowledge ('architecture') and human activities ('restoration of artworks').

The keywords that represent our Website should be chosen in accordance with the three main elements that define a site: its content, its objectives and its public – with a particular emphasis on this last element, that is, the public that the web for which the campaign is being devised targets.

It is recommended to start by searching for at least three or four principal concepts related to the site. For example, in the case of a film museum Website, the first words would be 'museum' and 'cinema'. Then it is necessary to derive from these words two or three synonyms and, hence, two or three more keywords, as well as some additional, more specific, keywords. Finally, some proper names should be added (eg, the name of the institution) and a place name if relevant (eg, if we wish to associate the museum with the city in which it is located).

It is important to involve the marketing department in this task if dealing with the site of a firm. Specifically, there are several procedures for helping to determine the keywords, although each has its pros and cons: expert analysis, frequency analysis, benchmarking, query analysis, analysis of the most searched words, traffic analysis and advertising tools.

- The analysis of the site by a human expert and/or using specific programs, such as IBP (www.ibusinesspromoter.com) as developed by Axandra. In this case, we obtain a list of the site's existing keywords, but we lose any perspective from outside the site. We also need to know which keywords we are not currently working with.
- A frequency analysis of the different keywords on the web related to the site and of their different synonyms using the search engines, some of which offer related searches. For example, both in Google and Bing, the search for 'earthquake' indicates as related searches 'tsunami' and 'hurricane', among others; Yahoo!, in response to this same search, proposes more specific responses like 'earthquake in Haiti'.
- Benchmarking to compare the keywords used by the Websites of our main competitors. In this case, it is very important to carefully define our competing SEO and to employ analytic tools like SEMRush (es. semrush.com/). Such tools allow us to see which keywords our competitors use to position themselves.

- The analysis of user queries, if our site has an internal search engine. This is usually a very powerful tool and yet one that is largely unexploited on most Websites. The analysis of our search engine query logs not only tells us which keywords our users employ but also what content they expect to find, something that should prove highly useful when prioritizing content creation.
- The analysis of the most searched words and of their respective variants, which can be obtained through the tools of some search engines, in particular, Google's search trend tool (Google Trends) http://www.google.com/trends/explore#cmpt=q.
- Of course, we can use web analytic tools, like Google Analytics, to see which keywords bring us traffic. Knowing these words usually constitutes a good starting point for understanding what our most attractive content is and how users search for us.
- But without doubt, the most effective tool for examining key words is Google AdWords (http://www.google.com/adwords/), or its competitor's equivalent Bing Ads (http://advertise.bingads.microsoft.com/es-es/inicio). They are tools that presuppose an advertising campaign, but they can be used even though we are not going to invest immediately in advertising. (In other units of this course, we will examine how they work in detail.)

Finally, we should mention the inverse process, in which we know the keywords before creating the Website, as might be the case, for example, when creating a site to sell or promote a particular product or service. Obviously in this case the keywords are determined a priori.

The outcome of the previous analyses should not only be a set of keywords but also two descriptive phrases of the site. The shorter of these two phrases is usually called the tagline. It normally appears in a prominent place on the site's homepage and is typically placed near the main title.

The tagline can be repeated on all the site's pages. This phrase forms part of the site's visible content. Not all sites consider it necessary to have a tagline (or at least, de facto, do not have one), but, in truth, the sites that use one can quickly inform first-time visitors what their site is about.

The second phrase forms part of the invisible content, that is, of the metadata, since it is used as content for the attribute description in the <meta description> tag in the source code, within the <head> section of the source code, and is considered essential because it is the part of the metadata that Google takes to build the results page (SERP) snippet.

As we have stressed already, SEO is applied at the page level. Therefore, the description on each of the site's pages might share a common element, for example, a common word to identify the company brand or the firm's name, but each page should have its own description to match its specific content.

We can also add keyword metadata, although Google insists that it has no impact on SEO. However, they are typically used for a variety of reasons: first, they can facilitate internal searches; and second, it would appear that other search engines, such as Bing, do use them.

Finally, each page should pay special attention to its <title> tag since, together with the <description> tag, these are the two elements of metadata that make up the main part of the snippet with which webpages are described on the SERP.

If the site is commencing its first positioning phase, but it is not a newly created site, but rather has been operating for months (or even years), a series of analyses of its potential should be carried out. Here, there are several possibilities open to us, but the most usual for making an initial diagnosis involve studies of the basic data concerning inbound links and the data provided by Google Webmaster Tools and Google Analytics, if the site is already registered and the administrator has opened an account. We shall return to these questions later on.

6.2.1.2 Competitor Analysis

No SEO analysis would be complete if we failed to compare our positioning with that of our main competitors. Several sites should be selected against which to measure our results. Just how many sites exactly is a question of time and budget, and also of just how fragmented and how competitive our market is. However, a comparison with at least three competing sites can be considered a good benchmark.

Using the free tools available (or if possible the paid versions, which tend to be much more complete), such as SEMRush, Moz, Majestic SEO, WooRank, Ahref and Alexa, provides us with key indicators for measuring various items of positioning, including:

- inbound links
- time spent on site
- bounce rate
- number of page views
- number of pages indexed
- position of competitors' pages for certain keywords
- social web: presence and interactions of competition in the social web

Some programs, like Moz, Majestic and Ahref, in addition, provide their own indicators, generally centred on concepts such as domain authority and domain or page reputation, based in turn on variations in their link analyses.

It is this competitor analysis that will tell us how successful we have been in our own actions. Likewise, repeating it at regular intervals (for example, once a month) should confirm whether we should maintain our current policies or if we need to think about introducing changes.

6.2.1.3 Information Architecture

The analysis of a site's information architecture, in relation to its SEO, should ensure that the navigation design and the choice of labelling meet the same quality standards as those that we presented in Chapter 2 of this book.

The reason for this is that a good architecture, in the shape of an efficient navigation system, has both direct and indirect influences on the SEO. It has a direct influence because it allows search engines to 'understand' and crawl the entire site. Therefore, the design of efficient global (or constant) and local navigation systems is critical.

But good architecture also has an indirect influence (and, moreover, one of utmost importance) because by facilitating the maximum usability of the site, its users will tend to stay longer on it, visiting more pages and making more recommendations about them on the social networks. All of this creates a set of user signals that are a decisive benefit for the SEO.

6.2.2 Design Phase

Our aim here is to present specific optimization proposals in relation to the various aspects under analysis. As far as the site content is concerned this means drawing up a policy for the creating and publishing of content centred on the site's themes, audience and objectives.

6.2.2.1 Content

The CISs, which are 'naturally' endowed with their own engine for content creation in virtue of their specific functions, need to optimize their content for keywords in line with the recommendations of the previous analyses. Moreover, they should also consider proposals on the following aspects:

- Planning the regular creation of quality content to post on the site and that links naturally to the site's keywords. For example, once a month (or each week) planning to publish a report on the different collections in the museum, which should include pictures; or organizing a cycle of annual conferences to be held in the museum and publishing the papers delivered, etc.

- Organizing the site's sections so that navigation means having to use the keywords in the site's menus.
- Using a system of subdirectories and file names that facilitate the use of the URL with keywords.
- Ensuring the top keywords appear in the file names of individual pages and in the names of the folders of the different site directories, so as to optimize the URL for positioning.
- Preparation of community building activities (community manager) centred on the site's publications.
- Ensuring that content production routines include elements of multimedia, in particular images, diagrams and, as far as possible, video.

6.2.2.2 Site Source Code

Search engines actually analyze and interpret a site's source code and not what we the users see via our browsers. Here again we need to bear in mind that the webpage is represented on the results page via the snippet, which, in turn, is made up from the <title> and <meta-description> tags. As such, to be effective, proposals need to focus on the use of web publishing standards and the attribute description.

As far as web publishing standards are concerned, HTML and CSS codes should be used. All attempts should be made to avoid obsolete forms of coding, such as sites created with Flash or other technologies that do not correspond to W3 Consortium recommended standards.

Likewise, use is recommended of the attribute description for the different <meta> elements, as well as for the content of the <title> tag in the <head> section of the homepage (and of the organization's other pages) and for the <author> attribute, if considered opportune to specify the name or names of the site's individual or corporate authors.

If, as is normally the case, the Website is created with a content management system, the configuration and page creation sections that generate these tags have to be identified. Often the <meta> and <title> tags are filled automatically using the information provided in the page or post titles. The <h1> and <h2> tags are also usually automatically generated when identifying the titles with WYSIWYG editor.

Similarly, the image alt attribute is filled when uploading an image with the editor. In each content management system, this operation has to be controlled to guarantee these basic positioning features.

In the case of some content management systems (like WordPress, for example), it is possible to add powerful plugins that provide full control of the two main components of the snippet, that is, the <title> and <description> tags.

6.2.3 Implementation Phase

Regardless of our SEO goal and strategy, and despite the loss of importance of *PageRank* discussed earlier, it remains essential to attract inbound links to ensure a good SEO. What's more, increasingly the best way to attract inbound links depends almost exclusively on the quality of the site's content.

However, it is always possible to obtain the first inbound links by adopting the following measures (recall that for the sake of simplicity we are considering the case of a site that is taking its first steps in SEO):

- Registering in thematic or regional directories and portals. A good starting point if we do not know any is to consult the Dmoz directory or to make thematic searches using Google and Bing.
- Attracting corporate links and links from similarly themed sites. In addition to the links our site might obtain from the aforementioned directories, we can almost certainly attract links from other sites, for example, from other Websites linked to our institution or sites with similar content (but it is always a good idea to show that we have already created the link).
- Creating accounts on social network sites. If we are serious about our presence on the social web, we must consider creating accounts with Pinterest, Facebook, LinkedIn, Twitter, Google Plus and Tumblr. We should also consider opening a channel on YouTube if we plan to create video content.
- Disseminating content via our accounts and channels in the aforementioned social networks. Ideally, a company should have a specific budget for promoting its content, including a community management program coordinated by a person dedicated to this activity, even if it is only part time.
- Creating one or more blogs (depending on the site's size and human resource capability) with site-related content, and a list of links to our site.

6.2.4 Monitoring Phase

Between the end of the campaign and conducting the first follow-up session, it is advisable to wait a while. Depending on the type of content and the tools used to create the Website, you might want to wait a few days or a few weeks. Often monitoring the results without waiting for the search engines to update their indexes can prove both frustrating and misleading. In general, the average time recommended is around a month.

In any case, once a certain period of time has elapsed since our latest SEO actions, it makes sense to check the results, first in the data from our own Google Analytics account and its equivalent in Bing.

Later, we should conduct the same analyses as outlined in phase 1 above, but this time the data should show some progress, particularly if we have focused our efforts on the OnSite SEO because, as we have stressed repeatedly, this, together with the inbound links, constitutes the most important factor. However, it is also something of a vicious circle, because according to the latest search engine algorithms, inbound links that are not obtained using quality content are worthless.

6.3 A FRAMEWORK FOR OPTIMIZING CONTENT ON INFORMATION-INTENSIVE SITES

According to Wikipedia, 'a framework is a standardized set of concepts, practices or criteria that allows us to focus on a particular type of problem and which serves as a reference for tackling and solving new problems of a similar nature'.

As we pointed out in Chapter 1, the most characteristic feature of CISs is that there is no need to develop any policies of content marketing or to implement any content strategies in order to attract the most important SEO factor, that is, an abundance of quality content with high social value.

Moreover, we know that the SEO factors used by search engines to calculate the relevance of a page in relation to a question fall into two broad categories: OffSite and OnSite.

In the previous chapter, we had the opportunity to discuss both categories in some detail. We were able to see that in modern SEOs the OnSite factors are, by far, the most important, for two converging factors: first, these are the factors that can be fully controlled by the site administrator; and, second, the most important of the OffSite factors, namely, the inbound links are directly related to the content.

As such, in the SEO that has been in use for at least the last five years (roughly since 2012 based on the family of Google algorithms known as Panda), content holds the key to search engine optimization, whether we are dealing with OnSite or OffSite factors.

The reason for this is quite simple. In the case of the OnSite factors, the keywords that make up part of the content constitute the basis for Website indexing and, therefore, for providing the search engines with their 'semantic understanding'.

As far as the OffSite factors are concerned, inbound links continue to be one of the most important factors, but search engines like Google no longer give the same value to all links. Indeed, some links might even have a negative value.

Today there are no shortcuts to obtaining quality inbound links; on the contrary, there is a broad consensus among companies specializing in SEO analyses (Searchmetrics and Moz, to name just two of the most important) that the only sure way to obtain these links is by creating quality content and the user experience of the Website's information architecture and navigation system.

Our objective in the following sections is to present a framework for the optimization of the content of a typical CIS (for example, a news media site) from the point of view of its SEO and social networks. To ensure a better understanding of the aspects of SEO analysis that we present in our proposal, we first need to define and consider some basic terminology: keyword, keyword density, optimal keyword density, SEO underoptimization, SEO overoptimization, optimal range, optimal distribution and latent semantic indexing.

- **Keyword**
  This is the term we expect internauts to use when searching for our news article, or alternatively we might say it is the term we hope that will make our article visible when used as a keyword in a Google search. Normally we optimize our news articles for a given keyword. If we want to optimize them for two or more keywords, then we need to reiterate the checks we present below.

- **Keyword density**
  This can be defined as the number of times the keyword occurs in relation to the total number of words in the news article. It is calculated by dividing the number of times the keyword occurs by the total word count and multiplying by 100. If in a 500-word article the keyword occurs 10 times, then it has a keyword density of 2%.

- **Optimal keyword density**
  Is there such a thing as an optimal density? Officially, Google assures us that there is not. The official doctrine is that we should write for humans, and not for Google, so that the optimal density is the one that natural language produces spontaneously. Some analyses claim that the density should not exceed 3%, while others fix 7% as the limit.

- **SEO underoptimization**
  Yet human beings are not always consistent. We can write a long article with the idea that we are focusing our discussion on a certain topic but in fact we barely use the keyword that best identifies it. And so the truth

is that a low number of repetitions of the keyword will prevent Google from considering our article relevant.

- **SEO overoptimization**

  At the same time, it is equally true that using the keyword too many times will mean the search engine will ignore it completely, given that the latest Google algorithms penalize SEO overoptimization.

- **Optimal range**

  So, if there is no optimal density, there does at least appear to be an optimal range that tells us what the minimum and maximum density would be. According to various analyses it seems to be relatively wide ranging from 0.5% to 2.5%.

- **Optimal distribution**

  Many SEO professionals prefer to think in terms of an optimal distribution rather than an optimal density. So what counts is *where* the keyword occurs – that is, where exactly on the page – and not the number of times it occurs. As long as we do not exceed the optimal range, the idea of the distribution is more efficient because it allows us to present a compelling structure from the outset without forcing the natural language.

- **Latent semantic indexing**

  This expression derives from information retrieval, that is, the theory on which search engines base themselves in order to 'understand' the topic of any given page. According to this theory, to know if a page is adequate for a certain keyword, we also need to consider the synonyms and related terms of that particular word. To determine whether a page is adequate for a search that uses the term 'human rights', the search engine will deem more relevant a page that, as well as containing the keyword, also contains such terms as 'democracy', 'freedom' or 'justice', among others.

6.3.1 Optimization Framework Scenario and Phases

In Section 6.2, for the purposes of conceptual clarity, we assumed the case of a site that was undertaking its first SEO campaign; likewise, here, and for the same motive, we will assume that we are working on a news media site. Therefore, in the following paragraphs, we assume that the CIS for which we are developing this optimization framework is the site of a social media outlet, such as, the Website of a travel magazine, or a magazine dedicated to politics, economics or gastronomy.

Based on these recommendations for designing a framework suitable for this type of CIS, the reader can extrapolate all, or nearly all, the framework features to other kinds of sites that, because of their content-intensive nature, need to publish content regularly, be it a newsletter or any other form of regular news content.

In any case, for this optimization framework, we assume it will be applied in three distinct phases:

- Writing of content – ideally, for an independent Website;
- SEO check – precisely what our framework considers;
- Publication and dissemination of the news article on the four major platforms: the Website itself, the SERP and the social networks of Twitter and Facebook.

6.3.2 Checkpoints

The application of our proposed framework for optimizing the content of a CIS requires adherence to a number of checkpoints following the writing of the content but before it is published. The points to consider are the following:

1. Length. The entry must have at least 300 words, and if possible it is better if it exceeds this figure.
2. Multimedia. Always incorporate elements of multimedia, at the very least a photograph.
3. Keyword. Decide what the principal keyword is for the entry.
4. Optimal distribution of the keyword:
   a. In the main heading or newspaper headline (h1 tag).
   b. In the URL entry. Edit the URL if necessary to avoid empty words and limit its length. Short, easily manageable titles are preferable.
   c. In the SEO title, through the <title> tag. Maximum 70 characters.
   d. In the metadata with the attribute description of the <meta> tag. Maximum 156 characters.
   e. In one of the headings in the body of the article (h2 tag).
   f. In the first paragraph.
   g. In some of the central paragraphs.
   h. In some of the final paragraphs.
   i. In one of the images.
   j. In any of the external hyperlinks to related sources.
5. Emphasis. In some of its occurrences, the keyword should be highlighted in bold or in italics.
6. Internal navigation. If possible, the keyword should link to an internal category or label.
7. Semantic support. Use synonyms and terms related to the keyword in the body and/or titles of the article to strengthen the keyword.

8. Credibility. Mention specific entities by referring to the names of people, places or institutions, and add links to the institutions if appropriate. This can serve to satisfy point 10 in the optimal distribution recommendations (number 4 in this list).

9. Internal links. Whenever possible, establish links with other thematically related entries, using your Website's system of labels or categories.

10. Social web. Be sure to configure the entry so that it can be published on the social networks, and incorporate buttons to share the article on your activated and configured social networks. If the possibility exists, consider if you wish to propose titles, descriptions and even specific images for platforms such as Facebook and Twitter.

11. Programming. Program the entry, if possible, so that it is published at the best time in relation to its content and nature.

6.4 CONCLUSIONS

In conclusion, we would like to reiterate the following points: positioning campaigns begin with the selection of the keywords and phrases that we want to use in optimizing our site for search engines.

Moreover, the site's content, which should be broad, original and enriched with multimedia components (photos, graphics, videos, diagrams, etc.), holds the key to site positioning, but certain optimization actions (such as those described in this chapter) can add value to this content with regard to search engines.

While multimedia components are important, our Website should always have text content accompanying the multimedia content: flash graphics and animations are of no use unless they are treated with meaningful metadata and file names.

The pages of our Website should also be optimized in terms of the source code and the metadata for the selected keywords. In today's web, only good content can help us obtain inbound links from third parties. Obtaining inbound links remains very important in ensuring the success of a positioning campaign. Additionally, updates, that is, the frequent supply of new content, are always an important factor as they serve to strengthen inbound links.

Finally, good content counts for little, at least in the short to medium term, unless we adopt an active policy of positioning, exploiting the social web and good community management activities.

CHAPTER 7

Mobile Web and SEO

7.1 INTRODUCTION

In earlier chapters we considered, first, the essentials of SEO and, second, the phases of an optimization campaign as well as a framework for optimizing the production of a content-intensive site (CIS), taking as our example a media communication site, although the recommendations we made can be extrapolated to other CISs. In this chapter, to conclude this section dedicated to SEO, we first review the current state of the mobile web, considering a range of different devices based on their screen size, given that this characteristic is the main determinant of the user experience. We also consider mobile operating systems and applications, in particular news aggregators. Finally, we link SEO and the mobile web via both searches and responsive web design, first introduced in Chapter 2.

7.2 MOBILE WEB ECOSYSTEM

There is little doubt that the desktop web (that is, the environment we access from our 'classical' computers) will continue to be important over the coming years and perhaps indefinitely. But there can be no doubt whatsoever that the mobile web is a fundamental part of the web and that it is only going to grow in importance in the future.

The following trend speaks volumes: the number of searches made from the mobile web is equal to or even greater than the number made from laptops or desktop computers, at least in many search categories, for example, transactional searches (eg, searches to find a restaurant in a given neighbourhood, or to find out the address and opening times of a museum). It is also true of a very specific type of informational search, for example, when we want answers to such questions as: Who directed the film '2001: A Space Odyssey'?, or, What year was such-and-such a film made?

We know that an ecosystem is characterized by the presence of a number of subsystems that compete with each other, but that also cooperate with each other, and in which there are various niches where each subsystem and its components live out their life cycle. In the case of the mobile web, there are at least three subsystems that we need to contemplate: the device (a combination of hardware and software), the operating system (software based) and the native mobile applications or apps.

7.2.1 Devices

The quintessential mobile devices are smartphones and tablets. There is another range of devices that have not yet acquired the same importance but it can only be a matter of time before they form an important part of the ecosystem. These are the so-called *wearables*, chief among which are smartwatches, activity trackers (usually wristbands that can measure activity-based data and track your health) and smart glasses. We shall speak more about the future of these wearables in the conclusion, because, as we say, their market presence is not yet comparable with that of smartphones and tablets.

7.2.1.1 Smartphones

The smartphone device started life as a mobile phone and, as such, is clearly an evolution of this device. However, they are being used less and less to make or receive voice calls, to the extent that even telephone operators are aware that this will become an increasingly smaller segment of their business (hence the diversification of their product portfolio into areas such as TV channels).

Currently, the inappropriately named *smartphone* is a combination of the following devices that previously required separate gadgets or appliances:

- mobile phone (we include it first, but it is becoming less and less important)
- tracker (measurement of health-related activities)
- video camera
- TV receiver
- sound recorder
- music system
- video player
- e-book reader
- newsstand
- Internet navigator
- portable office (email, diary, planner, etc.)

Focusing on the last two points in this list, what in part has allowed the smartphone to take the place of the laptop (which is being slowly replaced by both these and tablets), albeit with a mix of advantages and drawbacks, are three key factors that have come together in time over the last few years:

namely, power, screens and data plans. The processing power of today's high-end smartphones is similar to that of laptops a few years ago. Their screens have a level of definition and a reading comfort far superior to those of laptops, and they are increasingly comparable in quality to the printed page, until recently the unbeatable benchmark of quality. Finally, the operators' data plans offer large bandwidths at consumer rates (that is not to say exactly cheap, but at least affordable).

All this can be found in a device weighing no more than 150 g and that, because of its size, even in the case of the large-screen *phablets*, fits easily into a jacket or trouser pocket.

For all these reasons, smartphones are the leading lights of the mobile web (while we await the development of wearables), to the extent that they have undermined the importance of tablets, the device we consider in the next subsection.

As many aspects of the user experience of the mobile web are linked to the screen size, this is one of the aspects we now consider in order to understand its relevance for the mobile ecosystem.

Currently, the standard diagonal screen size of a medium- or high-end smartphone is about 5 in.

User experience is also closely linked to screen definition. The best quality resolutions lie somewhere between what is known as full high definition, which in a 5-inch screen provides more than 400 pixels per inch, and Quad HD, which exceeds 500 pixels on the same size screen.

The benchmark is 300 pixels per inch, considered the quality threshold. Below this threshold, the human eye can distinguish individual pixels and reading comfort decreases. However, this threshold is disputed and is highly controversial. The former president of Apple, Steve Jobs, claimed that at higher densities, the human eye is unable to perceive improvements in display resolution.

However, a number of leading specialists (Soneira, 2012) counter that this is only true at certain distances between the terminal and the human eye and that visual acuity can vary. They argue that the true threshold is much higher, with some identifying a value of 530 pixels. Interestingly, the Japanese manufacturer, Sony, has announced it is to launch a terminal in 2016 with a density of 800 pixels.

7.2.1.2 Tablets

Unlike smartphones, tablets do not have such an obvious precursor in the history of gadgets. If anything, they can be compared with laptops, but when they first emerged this comparison was not so obvious. Given their lack of a physical keyboard and the absence of most office applications, they initially appeared to be a genuine newcomer to the world of gadgets and devices.

However, the same improvements enjoyed by smartphones have gradually been applied to tablets, including the introduction of an increasing number of office applications. In addition, cases have been designed for tablets that allow users who want to use them as substitute laptops to incorporate a physical keyboard.

We can draw up virtually the same list of applications and utilities for tablets as we presented for smartphones (camera, video camera, e-book reader, etc.) with the exception of voice calls and associated applications, including various messaging applications.

However, even this has changed with the launch of tablets that can make and receive phone calls. Yet, in late 2015, the tablet market went into recession, a slump that continued into 2016, caused in all probability by the appearance of the phablets, which we review next.

If we continue to use the screen diagonal measurement as our differentiating criterion, then tablets range in size between 7 and 12 in. A single, standard size, however, is more difficult to define in the case of tablets, as they tend to fluctuate between 8 and 10 in.

7.2.1.3 Phablets

So where exactly does the boundary lie between smartphones and tablets? At the extremes of the spectra the distinction is clear. For example, between a smartphone with a 4-inch screen and a tablet with a 9.7- or 10.1-inch display there is a world of difference. Likewise, as mentioned, a clear distinction can be made in terms of the ability of smartphones to make voice calls.

However, given that we can find both 7-inch tablets and 6.2-inch smartphones, the distinction is not always so clear. To describe this emerging reality, the term *phablet* was coined, a portmanteau of the words phone and tablet.

A phablet therefore is used to describe devices that are bigger than 5 in., like the line of devices that typically have the word *note* in their name and are usually between 5.5 and 6 in.

Between 2014 and 2016, phablets enjoyed greater market acceptance than expected and seem to be cannibalizing both tablets (being, in part, responsible for their drop in sales), and, to some extent, laptops. Gradually, it seems that phablets are situating themselves as the true point of reference for the high-end mobile web.

If we examine them in terms of user experience, it seems logical that phablets (that is, devices with a diagonal display of 5.5 or more inches) should be winning favour among the most demanding users. Similar in size to smartphones (they can still be slipped into a pocket), thanks to a better exploitation of the ratio between the device's overall size and the screen size (currently around 80% on some models), they offer a much better user experience for productivity (planner and email, etc.) and leisure (photo and video) applications.

Their versatility, therefore, is much greater, offering in some cases similar functions to those of a laptop, that is, we can even edit office documents with a phablet, although clearly they are not the most suitable device for writing long documents. But they do allow the user to write and edit emails, manage their agenda, carry out small editing tasks on text documents or presentations, etc., tasks that until recently seemed limited to laptops. If to this we add the fact that we can read the press, look at photographs and videos in almost perfect conditions, then their acceptance is hardly strange despite initial reservations.

7.2.2 Operating Systems

There can, as we well know, be no hardware without software, at least if we are talking about things that carry the prefix *smart*. In the case of mobile web devices, the two main operating systems today are Android and iOS.

The first of these, Android, is in theory an open system. It is operated by a consortium of manufacturers, but its development is led by Google. It is, in some way, the dominant system in the market. It is used by hundreds of manufacturers worldwide and it enjoys an overwhelming presence in many countries of Europe, in China and, generally, throughout the Asian market. It has a reputation (probably deservedly so) of being the operating system that is best designed not solely for leisure and the consumption of information but also for productivity activities.

The second system, iOS, is a proprietary system developed by Apple and is the heart and soul of its tablets, iPad, and smartphones (iPhone). Although no longer the dominant system, Apple remains the leading mobile handset manufacturer in the world. In other words, it might not have the most common operating system any more, but Apple continues to be the world's leading manufacturer, producing more than Samsung and the other giants of mobile computing in Asia, the continent that concentrates the sector's main manufacturers. iOS had a reputation (possibly deservedly so) of being an operating system more closely centred on leisure and the consumption of information than on productivity. Clearly, this is no longer the case with the development of the latest versions presented during 2016. Of course, other operating systems exist, but they are either in decline (Blackberry) or never really got off the ground (Tizen, Firefox OS and Ubuntu).

The system that should have a bright future is **Windows**, produced by the giant maker of office automation software (and hardware), Microsoft. But since 2015 its market share has been in constant decline, falling to less than 3% in 2016. Its strong links with office automation suggest, however, that it is likely to regain market share in the future with the launch of Windows version 10, which unifies the operating system for phones, tablets and desktop. Indeed, the fairly successful Microsoft tablet-laptop hybrid, known as Surface, seems to be offsetting its disappointing performance in the smartphone sector.

7.2.3 Apps

In the mobile web ecosystem, smartphone and tablet applications are at the undisputed cutting edge of creativity in the design of interactive information systems.

In fact, we are currently experiencing a veritable explosion of creativity in user interface technology, user experience and the design of interactivity thanks to the solutions being implemented by these applications. It is the ideal terrain for professionals and students in these fields, as probably the best thinkers and designers in the world of interactivity are today working in the field of mobile applications.

7.2.3.1 Predictive Search

In the search engine field, however, we are witnesses to a virtual monopoly. Although various search apps are available both in the mobile web as in that of the desktop, one has come to dominate, namely, Google with Google Now, an application that is present in both major operating systems (Android and iOS).

The greatest innovation in this sense is that of the so-called 'predictive' search. Here, the search engine, Google in this case, does not wait for the user to make their search query, but by using cards, of which there are currently around 30, Google Now predicts and offers information via a notification system, or whenever the user opens the application, without their being any need to launch a search.

Although it might vary from one country to another, at the start of 2016, Google Now comprises, as we said, more than 30 cards meaning that the system is able to make predictions and inform the user on a multitude of subjects ranging from the weather and film premières to public transport timetables, traffic conditions, the results of their favourite teams and upcoming engagements in their diaries.

We have entered a new era of information, based without any question on the prodigious capacity of mobile devices to provide constant information about everything the user does, thanks to the GPS, Wi-Fi and the sensor system they incorporate. The ultimate goal of predictive search would be to provide 80% or 90% of the information needed by users in their everyday life without their having need to request it.

Monetization by Google will undoubtedly be linked to advertising. Every time we use Google Now, we provide the system with more information (though Google Now will not work if we have not activated an account). Thus, in theory, Google's advertising should become more and more relevant to the particular user, which is not necessarily a bad thing. Nobody wants to receive ads that are of no interest to them. The problem is if the advertising becomes very invasive or if this huge amount of data is misused.

7.2.3.2 Aggregators
News and current affairs aggregators are, right now, probably the most agile and sophisticated information systems for documents and multimedia yet to be developed.

In this sector, there is a wide range of solutions available to users. Following, by way of example, we identify the five information aggregator apps that are probably at the forefront of innovation today and that we need to be aware of if we want to have a good idea of how this sector is evolving. Specifically, we shall speak of the following five, each with at least versions for Android and iOS: Flipboard, Yahoo News Digest, News360, News Republic and Google Play Newsstand.

A common feature of all these applications is that they are able to connect with a wide variety of sources, categorizing and bringing them together to create complete press kits, updated daily or even several times a day. Some, notably Yahoo News, have the ability to aggregate in one newsworthy event or in the same story, news and information from diverse sources.

Flipboard provides a unique integration of news and of learning about the user's tastes and interests, skills taken from the magazine-style reading app it bought in 2014, Zite. At present, it is arguably the leading aggregation app and the one that would appear to have the brightest future given it is supported by the Android operating system, although it is also available in iOS and, in this latter case, the design is remarkably elegant and free of clutter. It provides one of the best user experiences for navigating its news page and offers a balanced layout of text, white spaces and images that make up the mosaic-like pages. Another leading aggregator is News Republic, an app that has been around for some time and that a few years ago seemed to have been eclipsed, but that is now going through something of a rejuvenation with a rich offer of national and international news sources.

Other notable aggregation applications, including Yahoo News Digest and News360, are no longer simply putting together thematic kits but complete and complex news items edited seamlessly from various sources. Clearly, we are witnesses to a whole new horizon in the world of information.

On the one hand, all these advances are placing an enormous wealth of information at the reach of users in ways hitherto unthinkable. On the other, they reinforce the idea that the content produced by the CISs, most notably the news media, does not have a clearly defined distribution platform but rather the content can appear on any platform that forms part of the web ecosystem, such as these aggregators, as well as on the social platforms in their mobile app versions. This leads us into the next section.

7.3 RESPONSIVE DESIGN

Until recently, the usual recommendation given with regard to SEO and the mobile web was to undertake a web analytics study. The aim of this was to determine whether, in view of the potential traffic from mobile devices, it was in the interests of the company to generate new versions of its site, or at least of some of its pages, for the mobile web. As part of the study, it was also recommended to determine whether the main devices used to access the site would be smartphones or tablets or other devices.

Currently, these recommendations are considered outdated. As we have noted, on the one hand, an increasing fraction of a site's traffic comes from mobile devices, regardless of the kind of site.

On the other hand, the vast majority of the population, in virtually the whole world, are users of smartphones, and the user behaviour of this population is multiscreen. This means that it is quite common for users to start browsing the web in the morning on their tablet, then, on their way to work, to continue their browsing via their smartphone, perhaps even in the same web. Once at work, they switch to a desktop computer, and then go back to their smartphone or tablet at home in the evening.

Therefore, it no longer makes sense to ask whether a site should be adapted to the mobile web because the mobile web is already very much part and parcel of the web. Google, well aware of this situation, announced that as of April 2015 it would give preference in its SERP to sites that were adapted to the mobile web. Google's obvious intention is to promote the sites that, if accessed by a search from a mobile device, are prepared for them. If we want to understand search engines, we must understand that their goal, so that they can retain their users, is always to rank those sites that provide the best user experience in the top places.

Another common recommendation used to be to evaluate which of the three main solutions (responsive design, selective presentation of pages or specific sites for mobiles) was the best for the company. Again, in this respect, search engines, and most particularly Google, have made their position quite clear: responsive design represents the optimal solution.

They are not alone in adopting this stance. Most web analysts and players, from the body that promotes its standards (W3C) to site designers and mobile web experts and scholars, support this option.

The reason why responsive design is the preferred solution is because, first, it is the solution that respects most closely the standards, since it is based on the use of HTML5 and CSS and on the philosophy of maintaining a strict separation between structure (HTML) and presentation (CSS); and, second, as noted in Chapter 2, it retains the standard URL address system, in which each page has a single URL, which is especially useful for the social web and its system of recommendations but also for preventing the web from filling up with duplicate content.

Creating new sites using responsive design should not necessarily require increased spending on development—probably just the opposite, as it should provide an effective protection of the investment made, since responsive sites by being based on official standards ensure better protection against new generations of devices and browsers.

Moreover, the strict separation that responsive sites impose between content and presentation is exactly the kind of solution that CISs need so that their naturally broad supply of content can be distributed to different screens (mobile web, desktop, etc.) and on various platforms (webpages, SERP and social networks, etc.) without their having to create distinct versions.

However, for existing sites with large volumes of content, the change can be costly in terms of both time and money (everything being a question of money in the end). For sites of this type, it is advisable to identify which pages are their landing pages on mobile devices and to focus all their rede-velopment efforts on these. But sooner rather than later, a strategy will have to be drawn up on how best to migrate their content to a responsive design. One such strategy would be to migrate the main page and the upper-level pages that depend on it, as well as the newly created content, to a responsive design, and to progressively go about the retrospective conversion of legacy content.

7.4 QUERY MODE AND TYPOLOGY

In addition to responsive design, the other great influence on SEO when considering the mobile web ecosystem is the query mode and user question typology.

As far as query mode is concerned, the mobile web has given a consider-able boost to improving our understanding of natural language searches by search engines. The reason for this lies in the use of voice as opposed to the keyboard to ask questions. This has led the search engines, most notably Google, to improve their ability to interpret the questions as a whole and not to rely solely on the use of keywords.

Indeed, some of the most recent changes in their algorithms have cen-tred on analyzing the users' search intent. The point is that, when we use voice (instead of the keyboard) to launch searches we tend to use more grammatical phrases than when we type. It is more frequent, in a voice search, for users to use natural language expressions such as 'how to get to the museum of modern art in New York', instead of typing keywords with-out indicating any syntactic relations between them, such as 'museum', 'modern art', etc.

This has led analysts in the world of SEO to recommend the production of content in which the titles also use these typical expressions from natural language, rather than using shorter titles or titles focused exclusively on the exploitation of keywords.

As for user intent, recall that in the desktop web three types of questions were dominant: navigational, transactional and informational. In the case of navigational questions, the user intent is to find a site's webpage without having to introduce the URL. Instead, the user typically employs a key-word, which usually comprises the name of the site or the most significant part of that name. For example, a navigational search query might involve introducing the name 'London' when searching for the city hall's Website instead of entering the exact URL. Transactional questions are those made with the intent of making a purchase in the short or medium term. Finally, informational questions are those made with the intent of learning or discovering more about a specific topic or field of knowledge.

The mobile web contributes at least two more types of questions to this scenario that those responsible for SEO need to consider. If we look at the guide published by Google for mobile web searches (Google, 2015), we need to add the following search types: 'do' queries, in which the user expects the device to perform a certain action, such as start a download. Such searches also include device action queries, and include the user's intention to get the device to perform some action, such as activate an app, for example, activating the agenda to note a reminder.

The second type are 'visit-in-person' queries, which include, as can easily be deduced from their name, the intent to personally visit a company or institution, for example, looking for the address of a museum before actually visiting it.

Although not enough time has yet elapsed for us to evaluate how exactly we can translate this new search scenario to a site's content strategies, a consensus has already been reached on at least four aspects that those responsible for a site should take into consideration in relation to SEO and the mobile web.

First and foremost is the philosophy, noted above, of 'mobile first', according to which new site design should be undertaken by putting the mobile web first, and only once the mobile design has been drawn up should the design be scaled up for the desktop. The same applies, of course, when redesigning an existing site.

Second, all sites should be properly geolocated. This, in turn, depends on two elements: first, there should be a credits or contacts page that clearly states the location of the head office or other offices of an institution. And, second, those institutions (such as universities and museums) for which personal visits are important should have a clear presence both in Google Maps and in Apple Maps through such systems as Google My Business and Yelp, respectively.

Third, the download and rendering speed of the pages in the browsers of both desktops and mobiles is also a positioning factor. Therefore, the site's source code and use of behavioural software, such as JavaScript, need to be optimized.

Fourth, the user experience must be as smooth and satisfactory in the mobile version as in the desktop version. This includes both the navigation as well as the use of forms, and of course, the use of readable typography on small screens and graphics that are adapted to these screens. The way to achieve this has already been discussed, since it depends on implementing the philosophy of 'mobile first', which, in turn, requires the use of responsive sites. Other important points include the ruling out of the use of plugins, such as Flash or the like, for animations or videos, as they can usefully be replaced by HTML5 components, and above all, avoiding intrusive advertisements that impede navigation.

7.5 CONCLUSIONS AND FUTURE PROSPECTS

The Internet of the future will have little in common with the one we have seen develop over the past decade, and this will not only be because of the enormous changes being induced by the mobile web. In addition to this, two new transformations, which seem set to converge, are underway: namely, the Internet of Wearables and the Internet of Things (IoT).

To date, the two best-known wearable devices are smartwatches and smart glasses, with Google Glass being the first on the market. But more gadgets are set to be launched linked both to the Internet of Wearables and the IoT, for example, shoes, shirts and bracelets, among others. To date, the wearable with apparently the most promising future is the smartwatch, thanks perhaps to the enormous influence of Apple for setting trends. Apple has launched its smartwatch, the iWatch, and the other major brands, including Samsung and Motorola, have either already developed their own models of smartwatches or recently launched one.

Part of the initial success of the smartwatch seems to be due to the fact it forms an excellent partnership with a smartphone. For the time being, its greatest function (other than that of telling the time with a precision that no mechanical watch can equal) seems to be linked to the delivery of notifications. Specifically, the user of a smartwatch can consult their watch for all (or almost all) the notifications on their mobile phone and interact (in part) with them, without having to get their mobile out of their pocket.

The smartwatch also has a number of other outstanding applications, including the ability to use it to remotely control a mobile camera or to follow the routes from the watch display when using such applications as Google Maps.

The IoT is likely to include physical objects that range from cars and home appliances to lighting systems and cutlery, which can all be connected to the Internet. Refrigerator sensors will be able to detect when an automatic order has to be placed to restock it with food at the supermarket.

It has been claimed that in the future even a lightbulb will have an IP address, and indeed this would appear to be the future. Literally everything, including the umbrella handle, can be connected to the Internet, so for example, an LED in its handle could be made to flash when it receives a warning of rain so that we do not forget to take it with us before leaving home.

The sector, however, in which the IoT is already being widely applied is that of automobiles, not only in the case of conventional cars, but also in the new wave of driverless cars. They, in all probability, will be just one more feature of our future smart cities, where traffic lights and other sensors will be connected via the Internet to help manage traffic and combat pollution.

As the IoT (or as it has been called, the Internet of Everything) is still in its infancy, we can only begin to speculate as to its potential. Here, we shall say no more other than to stress its undoubted interest for the future.

It is still too early to gauge the changes that these two new innovations will bring about, as they are only just beginning to hit the market, but together with the mobile web they will make up the changing landscape of the web in the coming years and information scholars and experts will have to pay very close attention to them.

Therefore, our final recommendations here are the need, first, to show a continued willingness to monitor all ongoing web trends; second, to adhere to a strict adaptation of W3C standards, since they are the best guarantee of all Website investments; and, third, to take a step toward responsive design on all those sites that have yet to adopt it, and of course, an unequivocal commitment not to pursue any new investment in the web that is not based on the philosophy of 'mobile first'.

Finally, we need to prepare ourselves for a new wave of changes ushered in by wearables and the IoT that will probably determine the landscape of the web, at least, over the next few years.

REFERENCES AND FURTHER READING

Ashworth, C., & Hamilton, D. (1997). A case for frames. In *Proceedings of the 3rd conference on human factors and the web*.

Barker, I. (2005). *Information scent: Helping people find the content they want.* [Online] Step Two Designs. http://www.steptwo.com.au/papers/kmc_informationscent.

Badre, A. N. (2002). *Shaping web usability: Interaction design in context.* Boston: Addison Wesley Professional.

Bailey, R. (2000). *Link affordance.* [Online] http://www.webusability.com.

Bailey, R., Koyani, S., & Nall, J. (2000). *Usability testing of several health information web sites.* Bethesda, MD: National Cancer Institute. Technical Report.

Banga, C. (2014). *Essential mobile interaction design: Perfecting interface design in mobile apps.* Boston: Addison-Wesley.

Bernard, M. (2001). *Developing schemas for the location of common web objects.* [Online] Usability News. http://psychology.wichita.edu/surl/usabilitynews/3W/web_object.htm.

Bernard, M. (2002). *Examining user expectations for the location of common e-commerce web objects.* [Online] Usability News. http://psychology.wichita.edu/surl/usabilitynews/41/web_object-ecom.htm.

Bernard, M., Hull, S., & Drake, D. (2001). *Where should you put the links? A comparison of four locations.* [Online] Usability News, 3.2. http://psychology.wichita.edu/surl/usabilitynews/3S/links.htm.

Bernard, M., & Larsen, L. (2001). *What is the best layout for multiple-column web pages?* Usability News.

Bieber, M. (1997). Enhancing information comprehension through hypertext. In C. Nicholas, & J. Mayfield (Eds.), *Intelligent hypertext: Advanced techniques for the world wide web.* Berlin: Springer-Verlag.

Billingsley, P. (1982). Navigation through hierarchical menu structures: does it help to have a map? In *Human factors and ergonomics society annual meeting proceedings* (pp. 103–107).

Blomquist, A., & Arvola, M. (2002). *Personas in action: Ethnography in an interaction design team.* Personas in Action: Ethnography in an Interaction Design Team. Aarhus, Denmark.

Bouch, A., Kuchinsky, A., & Bhatti, N. (2000). Quality is in the eye of the beholder: meeting users' requirements for internet quality of service. In *Proceedings of CHI 2000* (pp. 297–304).

Bovair, S., Kieras, D., & Polson, P. G. (1990). The acquisition and performance of text-editing skill: a cognitive complexity analysis. *Human-Computer Interaction, 5*(1), 1–48.

Brown, D. (2010). *Communicating design: developing web site documentation and planning.* Berkeley: New Riders.

Budiu, R., & Nielsen, J. (2012). *Mobile usability.* San Francisco: New Riders Press.

Byrne, M., Anderson, J., Douglass, S., & Matessa, M. (1999). Eye tracking the visual search of click-down menus. In *Proceedings of CHI'99* (pp. 402–409).

Byrne, M., John, B., Wehrle, N., & Crow, D. (1999). The tangled web we wove: a taskonomy of WWW use. In *Proceedings of CHI'99* (pp. 544–551).

Card, S., Pirolli, P., van Der Wege, M., Morrison, J., Reeder, R., Schraedley, P., et al. (2001). Information scent as a driver of web behaviour graphs: results of a protocol analysis method for web usability. In *Proceedings of CHI 2001* (pp. 498–505).

Chaparro, B., Minnaert, G., & Phipps, C. (2000). Limitations of using mouse-over with menu item selection. In *Human factors and ergonomics society annual meeting proceedings*.

Chapman, C. N., & Milham, R. P. (2006). The personas' new clothes: methodological and practical arguments against a popular method. In *Human factors and ergonomics society 50th annual meeting* (pp. 634–636).

Chi, E., Pirolli, P., Chen, K., & Pitkow, J. (2001). Using information scent to model user information needs and actions on the web. In *Proceedings of the ACM conference on human factors in computing systems* (pp. 490–497).

Chu, H. (2003). *Information representation and retrieval in the digital age.* Medford: Information Today.

Cooper, A. (1999). *The inmates are running the asylum: Why high tech products drive us crazy and how to restore the sanity.* Indianapolis: Sams Publishing.

Covi, L., & Ackerman, M. (1995). Such easy-to-use systems! How organizations shape the design and use of online help systems. In *Proceedings of conference on organizational computing systems* (pp. 280–288).

Czaja, S., & Sharit, J. (1997). The influence of age and experience on the performance of a data entry task. In *Human factors and ergonomics society annual meeting proceedings* (pp. 144–147).

Detweiler, M., & Omanson, R. (1996). *Ameritech web page user interface standards and design guidelines.* [Online] http://www05.sbc.com/news/testtown/library/standard/web_guidelines/index.html.

Dias, P., & Sousa, A. (1997). Understanding navigation and disorientation in hypermedia learning environments. *Journal of Educational Multimedia and Hypermedia, 6,* 173–185.

Ehret, B. D. (2002). Learning where to look: location learning in graphical user interfaces. In *CHI 2002 conference proceedings* (pp. 211–218).

Enge, E., Spencer, S., Stricchiola, J., & Fishkin, R. (2015). *The art of SEO.* Sebastopol: O'Reilly.

Evans, M. (1998). *Web design: An empiricist's guide.* Unpublished master's thesis. [Online] Seattle: University of Washington. http://response.restoration.noaa.gov/webmastr/webdesgn.pdf.l.

Farkas, D., & Farkas, J. (2000). Guidelines for designing web navigation. *Technical Communication, 47*(3), 341–358.

Farris, J., Jones, K., & Elgin, P. (2001). Mental representations of hypermedia: an evaluation of the spatial assumption. In *Human factors and ergonomics society annual meeting proceedings* (pp. 1156–1160).

Fleischner, M., & Michael, H. (2011). *SEO made simple: Strategies for dominating the world's largest search engine.* CreateSpace Independent Publishing.

Fling, B. (2009). *Mobile design and development: practical concepts and techniques for creating mobile sites and web apps.* Sebastopol (CA): O'Reilly Media Inc.

Foltz, P., Davies, S., Polson, P., & Kieras, D. (1988). Transfer between menu systems. In *Proceedings of CHI'88* (pp. 107–112).

Freixa, P., Ribas, J. I., & Codina, L. (2015). Comparative analysis of mobile web applications for the main international news agencies: state of the art and preliminary results. In K. Meso, I. Agirreazkuenaga, & A. Larrondo (Eds.), *Active audiences and journalism* (pp. 143–162). Bilbao: Univ. País Vasco.

Freixa, P., Soler-Adillon, J., Sora, C., & Ribas, J. I. (2014). *Contributions of the interactive decoupage to reading and analyzing interactive audiovisual works in cybermedia.* Hipertext.net. [Online] 12.

Garrett, J. J. (2010). *The elements of user experience.* Berkeley: New Riders.

Gerhardt-Powals, J. (1996). Cognitive engineering principles for enhancing human-computer performance. *International Journal of Human-Computer Interaction, 8*(2), 189–211.

Google. (2015). *Search quality rating guidelines.* https://static.googleusercontent.com/media/www.google.com/es//insidesearch/howsearchworks/assets/searchqualityevaluatorguidelines.pdf.

Guallar, J., & Abadal, E. (2010). The digital press archives of the leading Spanish online newspapers. *Information Research, 15*(1).

Gube, J. (2009). *Breadcrumbs in web design: examples and best practices.* [Online] Smashing Magazine. http://www.smashingmagazine.com/2009/03/17/breadcrumbs-in-web-design-examples-and-best-practices-2/.

Gudjonsdottir, R., & Lindquist, S. (2008). Personas and scenarios: design tool or a communication device? In *Proceedings of 8th international conference on the design of cooperative systems* (pp. 165–176).

Haas, S., & Grams, E. (1998). A link taxonomy for web pages. In *Proceedings of the 61st annual meeting of the American society for information science* (pp. 485–495).

Hamm, M. (2014). *Wireframing essentials*. Birmingham: Packt Publishing.

Hornof, A., & Halverson, T. (2003). Cognitive strategies and eye movements for searching hierarchical computer displays. In *CHI 2003 conference proceedings* (pp. 249–256).

IBM. (1999). *Web design guidelines design in action*. [Online] www-3.ibm.com/ibm/easy/eou_ ext.nsf/Publish/572.

Instone, K. (2009). *Location, path & attribute breadcrumbs*. [Online] http://instone.org/breadcrumbs.

Ivory, M., Sinha, R., & Hearst, M. (2000). Preliminary findings on quantitative measures for distinguishing highly rated information-centric web pages. [Online] In *Proceedings of the 6th conference on human factors and the web*. http://www.tri.sbc.com/hfweb/ivory/ paper.html.

Kalbach, J. (2007). *Designing web navigation*. Sebastopol (CA): O'Reilly Media Inc.

Kandogan, E., & Shneiderman, B. (1997). Elastic windows: a hierarchical multi-window world-wide web browser. In *Proceedings of the 10th annual ACM symposium on user interface software and technology* (pp. 169–177).

Katz, M., & Byrne, M. (2003). Effects of scent and breadth on use of site-specific search on e-commerce web sites. *ACM Transactions on Computer-Human Interaction, 10*(3), 198–220.

Kieras, D. (1997). A guide to GOMS model usability evaluation using NGOMSL. In M. Helander, T. Landauer, & P. Prabhu (Eds.), *Handbook of human-computer interaction*. Amsterdam: North-Holland Elsevier Science Publishers.

Kim, H., & Hirtle, S. C. (1995). Spatial metaphors and orientation in hypertext browsing. *Behaviour and Information Technology, 14*, 239–250.

Kingsburg, J., & Andre, A. (2004). A comparison of three-level web menus: navigation structures. In *Proceedings of the human factors and ergonomics society 48th annual meeting*.

Koch, P.-P. (2014). *The mobile web handbook*. Freiburg: Smashing Magazine GmbH.

Kowalski, G. (1997). Automatic indexing. In *Information retrieval systems: Theory and implementation*. Boston: Kluwer.

Koyani, S., & Nall, J. (1999). *Web site design and usability guidelines*. Bethesda, MD: National Cancer Institute. Communication Technologies Branch Technical Report.

Krug, S. (2000). *Don't make me think: A common sense approach to web usability*. Indianapolis, IN: New Riders.

Larrondo, A., Diaz Noci, J. (2014). Hypertextual structure of online news: a comparative research on quality media. In A. Larrondo, K. Meso, A. Tous (Coords). *Shapping the news online. A comparative research on international quality media* (pp. 249–300). Covilhã: Livros LabCom.

Levine, R. (1996). *Guide to web style*. Sun Microsystems.

Lidwell, W., Holden, K., & Butler, J. (2003). *Universal principles of design*. Beverly: Rockport Publishers.

Liu, B. (2007). Information retrieval and web search. In *Web data mining: Exploring hyperlinks, contents, and usage data*. Berlin: Springer.

Lynch, P., & Horton, S. (2009). *Web style guide: basic design principles for creating web sites*. New Haven (CT): Yale University Press.

Marchionini, G. (1995). *Information seeking in electronic environments*. New York: Cambridge University Press.

Marcotte, E. (2010). *Responsive web design*. [Online] http://alistapart.com/article/responsive-web-design.

McCallister, J. (2014). *Mobile apps made simple: The ultimate guide to quickly creating, designing and utilizing mobile apps for your business*. Seattle: CreateSpace.

McDonald, S., & Stevenson, R. (1998). Navigation in hyperspace: an evaluation of the effects of navigational tools and subject matter expertise on browsing and information retrieval in hypertext. *Interacting with Computers, 10,* 129–142.

McEneaney, J. (2001). Graphic and numerical methods to assess navigation in hypertext. *International Journal of Human-Computer Studies, 55,* 761–766.

McNeil, P. (2012). *The designer's web handbook: What you need to know to create for the web.* Cincinnati: HOW Books.

McVicar, E. (2012). *Designing for mobile: Information architecture.* [Online] http://www.uxboot h.com/articles/designing-for-mobile-part-1-information-architecture.

Meso, K., Agirreazkuenaga, I., & Larrondo, A. (Eds.). (2015). *Active audiences and journalism: Analysis of the quality and regulation of the user generated contents.* Bilbao: Univ. País Vasco.

Meyer, J., Shinar, D., & Leiser, D. (1997). Multiple factors that determine performance with tables and graphs. *Human Factors, 39*(2), 268–286.

Monefa, N. (2015). *Apps: The ultimate beginners guide for app programming and development.* Paramount: Paramount Publishing Company.

Moray, N., & Butler, C. (2000). The effect of different styles of human-machine interaction on the nature of operator mental models. In *Human factors and ergonomics society annual meeting proceedings* (pp. 1–56).

Morrell, R., Dailey, S., Feldman, C., Mayhorn, C., & Echt, K.V. (2002). *Older adults and information technology: A compendium of scientific research and web site accessibility guidelines.* Bethesda, MD: National Institute on Aging Report.

Morville, P., Rosenfeld, L., & Arango, J. (2015). *Information architecture for the web and beyond.* Sebastopol (CA): O'Reilly Media Inc.

Nall, J., Koyani, S., & Lafond, C. (2001). *Lessons learned while usability testing the CancerNet web site.* National Cancer Institute. Communication Technologies Branch Technical Report.

Neil, T. (2014). *Mobile desing pattern gallery.* Sebastopol (CA): O'Reilly Media Inc.

Nielsen, J. (1990). The art of navigating through hypertext. *Communications of the ACM, 33*(3), 296–310.

Nielsen, J. (1996). *Top ten mistakes in web design.* [Online] http://www.useit.com/alertbox/9 605.html.

Nielsen, J. (1997). *The need for speed.* [Online] http://www.useit.com/alertbox/9703a.html.

Nielsen, J. (1999a). *'Top ten mistakes' revisited three years later.* [Online] http://www.useit.com/ alertbox/990502.html.

Nielsen, J. (1999b). *The top ten new mistakes of web design.* [Online] http://www.useit.com/al ertbox/990530.html.

Nielsen, J. (1999c). *Ten good deeds in web design.* [Online] http://www.useit.com/alertbox/99 1003.html.

Nielsen, J. (2003). *The ten most violated homepage design guidelines.* [Online] http://www.useit. com/alertbox/20031110.html.

Nielsen, J. (2009). *Top 10 information architecture mistakes.* [Online] http://www.useit.com/ alertbox/ia-mistakes.html.

Nielsen, J. (2014). *An era of growth: The cross-platform report.* [Online] http://www.nielsen. com/us/en/reports/2014/an-era-of-growth-the-cross-platform-report.html.

Nielsen, J., & Tahir, M. (2002). *Homepage usability: 50 sites deconstructed.* Indianapolis: New Riders Publishing.

Niemela, M., & Saarinen, J. (2000). Visual Search for Grouped versus Ungrouped Icons in a Computer Interface. *Human Factors, 42*(4), 630–635.

Palacios, M., & Díaz-Noci, J. (2009). *Online journalism: Research methods. A multidisciplinary approach in comparative perspective.* Editorial Univ. País Vasco.

Piolat, A., Roussey, J., & Thunin, O. (1998). Effects of screen presentation on text reading and revising. *International Journal of Human Computer Studies, 47,* 565–589.

Pirolli, P., & Card, S. (1995). Information foraging in information access environments. In *Proceedings of the conference on human factors in computing* (pp. 51–58).

Pirolli, P., Card, S., & van Der Wege, M. (2000). The effects of information scent on searching information visualizations of large tree structures. In *Proceedings of the working conference on advanced visual interfaces* (pp. 161–172).

Plaisant, C., Marchionini, G., Bruns, T., Komlodi, A., & Campbell, L. (1997). Bringing treasures to the surface: iterative design for the library of congress national digital library program. In *Proceedings of CHI'97* (pp. 518–525).

Polson, P., Bovair, S., & Kieras, D. (1987). Transfer between text editors: predictive cognitive modelling. In *Proceedings of CHI+GI'87* (pp. 27–32).

Polson, P., & Kieras, D. (1985). A quantitative model of the learning and performance of text editing knowledge. In *Proceedings of CHI'85* (pp. 207–212).

Polson, P., Muncher, E., & Engelbeck, G. (1986). A test of a common elements theory of transfer. In *Proceedings of CHI'86* (pp. 78–83).

Porter, J. (2003). *Testing the three-click rule.* [Online] User Interface Engineering. http://www.uie.com/articles/three_click_rule/.

Purewal, S. (2014). *Learning web app development.* Sebastopol (CA): O'Reilly Media Inc.

Ramos, A., & Cota, S. (2006). *Insider SEO & Ppc: Get your Website to the Top of the Search Engines.* Fremont (CA): Jain Pub Co.

Rönkkö, K. (2005). An empirical study demonstrating how different design constraints, project organization, and contexts limited the utility of personas. In *Paper presented at Hawaii international conference on system sciences 2005, Waikoloa, HI.*

Rönkkö, K., Hellman, M., Kilander, B., & Dittrich, Y. (2004). Personas is not applicable: local remedies interpreted in a wider context. In *Paper presented at participatory design conference 2004, Toronto, ON.*

Schwarz, E., Beldie, I., & Pastoor, S. (1983). A comparison of paging and scrolling for changing screen contents by inexperienced users. *Human Factors, 24,* 279–282.

Sharpe, I. (2015). *Apps: App design and app development made simple.* Seattle: CreateSpace.

Sheridan, T. (1997). Supervisory control. In G. Salvendy (Ed.), *Handbook of human factors.* New York: Wiley.

Smith, J., Bubb-Lewis, C., & Suh, Y. (2000). Taking order status to task: improving usability on the ibuy lucent web site. In *Proceedings of the 6th conference on human factors and the web.*

Smith, S., & Mosier, J. (1986). *Guidelines for designing user interface software.* The *MITRE Corporation Technical Report* (ESD-TR-86-278).

Sonderegger, P., Manning, H., Souza, R., Goldman, H., & Dalton, J. (1999). *Why most B-to-B sites fail.* Forester Research.

Soneira, R. (2012). New iPad Display Technology Shoot-Out. *DisplaMate.* [Online] http://www.displaymate.com/iPad_ShootOut_1.htm>. [Retrieved: 1 November 2015].

Spain, K. (1999). *What's the best way to wrap links?* [Online] Usability News. http://psychology.wichita.edu/surl/usabilitynews/1w/Links.htm.

Spool, J., Klee, M., & Schroeder, W. (2000). *Report 3: Designing for scent, designing information-rich web sites.* Bradford: User Interface Engineering.

Spool, J., Scanlon, T., Schroeder, W., Snyder, C., & DeAngelo, T. (1997). *Web site usability: A designer's guide.* North Andover: User Interface Engineering.

Spool, J., Schroeder, W., & Ojakaar, E. (2001). *Users don't learn to search better.* [Online] UIEtips. http://www.uie.com/articles/learn_to_search.

Spyridakis, J. H. (2000). Guidelines for authoring comprehensible web pages and evaluating their success. *Technical Communication, 47*(3), 359–382.

Stanton, N., Taylor, R., & Tweedie, L. (1992). Maps as navigational aids in hypertext environments: an empirical evaluation. *Journal of Educational Multimedia and Hypermedia, 1,* 431–444.

Suau, J., & Masip, P. (2015). Models of online media participation and active audiences. A comparison of what the media are offering and what citizens are looking for. In K. Meso, I. Agirreazkuenaga, & A. Larrondo (Eds.), *Active audiences and journalism* (pp. 119–142). Bilbao: Univ. País Vasco.

Tullis, T. S. (2001). *Web usability lessons learned* Fidelity Center for Applied Technology Technical Report. Fidelity Investments.

Utting, K., & Yankelovich, N. (1989). Context and orientation hypermedia networks. *ACM Transactions on Office Information Systems*, *7*, 57–84.

Vállez, M., Pedraza-Jiménez, R., Codina, L., Blanco, S., & Rovira, C. (2015). A semi-automatic indexing system based on embedded information in HTML documents. *Library Hi Tech*, *33*(2), 195–210.

W3C. (2005). *Scope of mobile web best practices.* [Online] http://www.w3.org/TR/2005/WD-mobile-bp-scope-20050901.

W3C. (2008). *Mobile web best practices.* [Online] http://www.w3.org/TR/mobile-bp/#OneWeb.

Williams, T. (2000). Guidelines for designing and evaluating the display of information on the web. *Technical Communication*, *47*(3), 383–396.

Wodtke, C. (2009). *Information architecture: blueprints for the web.* Boston: New Riders Publishing.

Wroblewski, L. (2009). *Mobile first.* [Online] http://www.lukew.com/ff/entry.asp?933.

Zaphiris, P. G. (2000). Depth versus breadth in the arrangement of web links. In *Proceedings of the 44th meeting of human factors and ergonomics society* (pp. 139–144).

Ziegler, J., Hoppe, H., & Fahnrich, K. (1986). Learning and transfer for text and graphics editing with a direct manipulation interface: transfer of user skill between systems. In *Proceedings of CHI'86* (pp. 72–77).

Zimmerman, D., Slater, M., & Kendall, P. (2001). Risk communication and a usability case study: implications for web site design. In *Proceedings of the IEEE international professional communication conference* (pp. 445–452).

INDEX

Printed and bound by CPI Group (UK) Ltd, Croydon, CR0 4YY

08/06/2025

01896869-0009